MADGE RUIZ

THE POWER OF STOICISM

Unleashing Resilience and Inner Strength
for a Fulfilling Life
(2023 Guide for Beginners)

Contents

INTRODUCTION

'Begin to live at once, and consider each separate day a separate life. He who has prepared himself that way, whose life every day is a rounded whole, is easy in his mind.' – Seneca.

Seneca had just completed discussing a guy he knew who had transformed his life from rags to riches when he wrote about treating each day as a separate existence. An acquaintance of Seneca had invested

He spent the majority of his life working to rise from poverty to prominence and was just starting to enjoy the benefits of his efforts when he passed away abruptly.

I initially realized that nothing in life is certain when I heard this story. We are constrained by our mortality. I realized it is silly to be careless and believe we have endless time to create elaborate arrangements for the wonderful life we would someday have. I'm not sure about you, but for a very long time every time a new year started, I would make big plans for the far-off future. Only around one of the plans actually materialized in the greatest year.

What I didn't grasp is that while setting specific objectives and plans for the future is important, until those plans turn into everyday routines, all of your efforts will be useless. This is so because our daily activities determine how our lives are lived. Seneca continued by saying that the better way to live is to set big goals for each and every day and make them all count. the notion? You can have a terrific year and a great life if you accumulate enough quality days and live them well. That concept was mind-blowing to me. But it did not result in the shift in my life that I had wanted. not yet, at least. I was still unhappy and dissatisfied with my life. That information hadn't yet entered my body, so it was still only a rumor.

I remember thinking when I was little that people used their thoughts as accessories to enhance their social personas. If you were an anarchist, for instance, like one teen lad I met, there was a statement to make. Whatever the concept, it seemed to me to be merely a name, something trivial. Naturally, I didn't consider life in those terms. Although I was too young and undeveloped, I was aware of my lack of interest in those things. Labels simply didn't interest me.

Maybe I got the impression that most of it was bluster. In any event, I made the decision to begin reading ancient novels. I reasoned that the viewpoint would be genuinely different if I read material that was written many years ago. It would go beyond what is conventionally allowed.

I came upon Marcus Aurelius' Meditations around that time, and it completely changed my perspective. I connected with the book in some way. I studied the stoics and learned about philosophy. I took in as much as I could, and of course, seemingly by accident, my life transformed and took on a direction I had always desired but had not been able to achieve up until that point. I started to use stoicism as a compass. It turned became my survival manual. Lack of emotional control was one of the defining characteristics of my existence at the time. My decisions were always affected by my emotions, and they were never the proper ones. The only difference between myself and an emotional hazard sign was that I was not constrained by any human law, social norm, or conscience. A sacrifice had to be made. There had to be a method to manage the stress, worry, dread, despair, and rage. There had to be a way out of all my pain. There had to be tranquility.

You see, every one of us possesses a library or perhaps an encyclopedia of knowledge within our brains. Our views, beliefs, and values are shaped by a wide range of events, lessons, and observations.

Some of this knowledge is true, but other parts are generalizations, presumptions, and beliefs that we have because we believe those who informed us. As a result, not all of our beliefs are beneficial to our health. Some of us, however, never stop to think about our beliefs or make an effort to better our lives. Choosing what you will believe and live by is part of adopting stoicism, which involves putting those beliefs into conscious thought. It involves sifting through the vast soup of viewpoints and concepts in your mind and discarding what you do not need.

If this sounds a little confusing, perhaps some stoics can clarify.

The soul is colored by the thoughts that it has, according to a statement made by Marcus Aurelius. Epictetus, another stoic, noted that mankind is only troubled by things as a result of the way they see them. The stoics discovered a human connection. They realized how much power our imaginations possess over how we live. The camera is to the quality of a picture and what the intellect is to our existence. A bad image results from a filthy lens. Suffering occurs from a negative belief-filled mind. Our experiences of life are influenced by the narratives we live out and the values we uphold.

Fortunately, we have the ability to alter our beliefs, which will alter our experiences. We have the knowledge we need to move closer to leading a good life thanks to the generous library of stoic works. Stoicism gives a foundation for living effectively in any condition or stage of life, at all times. It serves as a reminder of what is actually important while also offering doable solutions for doing more of what is worthwhile. You don't need to acquire a new philosophical vocabulary to practice stoicism because the philosophy was created to be practical, accessible, and actionable. It gives a quick and useful technique to achieve tranquility and strengthen your character.

If you understand what it's like to be dissatisfied with your life, this book is for you. If you detest being controlled by bad feelings and thoughts, it's for you. You will discover how to handle major life emotions here. You'll realize how rage may be your ally. You will learn how to harness your fear, grief, and anxiety. You will learn how the wise men of old ran their lives in this book, along with the values and concepts that gave them the power they did. By the end of this book, hopefully, you won't allow your feelings to dictate how you act or how you perceive the world.

Your main worry might not be that your feelings affect your choice so much as they seem to steal your tranquility. Maybe anxiousness robs your peace of mind every time you decide on a direction in life. You can benefit from this book, too. You'll learn how to put an end to fretting about things you can't change. You'll discover how to concentrate on the things you can control. You will discover how to find the fortitude to go forward, beyond the setback, and into the space you want to be in. As a result, depression and anxiety will no longer rule your life. You'll be amazed at how well-adjusted and clear your mind is when you complete this.

You will be able to tell what is a story from what is true by the time you finish this book. We typically suffer when our beliefs and the stories we accept become rigid and when we erroneously equate fiction with reality. These rigid narratives don't allow for conflicting evidence, making us irritated, defensive, unreasonable, and intolerable. Your beliefs won't be rigid after reading this book, I promise. You'll develop your fluidity and ability to, as they say, "roll with the punches." But this book will also ask you to do something. It will need that you be willing to reflect on yourself. It is up to you to examine your beliefs and determine whether they are assisting you or hindering you.

Many of the books I read when I first started learning about stoicism were unhelpful. The majority of them were either too general, convoluted, or scholarly to be of much use. Others felt like a flowery self-help book or were just too much for someone who was new to stoicism. I made an effort to make this book unique. In addition to inspiring me to write this book, my love of stoicism inspired me to create each chapter and component of it with the intention of assisting you in implementing true stoicism in your life.

The suggestions you'll find here are applicable and tailored to our contemporary environment and problems. This book is purposely modern, yet it also has very strong roots in traditional stoicism. Being a part of the resurgence of stoic principles is one of my objectives in publishing books like this. I envision a future where my work has the power to influence and transform the lives of millions, enabling you to be happier and have more mental control.

Along with my ardent love of stoicism, I have a BA in Behavioral Psychology and an MA in Philosophy, which have a significant impact on how I apply stoicism to contemporary life difficulties. For many years, I worked as a coach and therapist, and I had the honor of assisting many of my clients as they sought to incorporate stoicism into their life. I've seen how stoic principles have transformed people's thoughts and lives, so I'm eager to do the same with this book. I currently reside in North Carolina with my best friend, our two kids, and our dog. I've been successful in achieving goals I never imagined for my life. I've been all over. I've even scaled Mount Kilimanjaro in Tanzania and Mount Denali in Alaska, and I eagerly anticipate more amazing journeys in my life. The stoic principles I will present in this book are the only ones that have made these things feasible. I owe them in a lot of ways to the finding of Marcus Aurelius' Meditations. You'll do well to remember them and put them into practice.

This book is broken into four sections. In the first section, it is discussed how morality and self-control can lead to happiness. You will change from pursuing happiness as the final goal of all your efforts, which is self-indulgent and short-sighted, to pursuing discipline and virtue, which results in happiness as a byproduct. The second section discusses controlling your emotions. You can learn here how the stoics handled theirs and how their insight can benefit you right now. You'll be able to care less thanks to part three. You'll be able to harness the power of indifference, and part four will assist you in developing mental discipline. By addressing the factors that contribute to your misery, I hope to offer a long-lasting solution to your suffering. Continue reading if this seems like the reason you are here.

HOW TO BE A STOIC LIKE EPICTETUS - WHAT CAN YOU CONTROL?

'No great thing is created suddenly, any more than a bunch of grapes. If you tell me that you want grapes, I answer that there must be time. Let the grave vine blossom, then bear fruit, then ripen.' – Epictetus.

Today, stoicism can be practiced to varying degrees. Some people say that you must adopt a stoic attitude and spend your life meticulously in their footsteps. Although that is one option, I have discovered that it is not the only one. Even if you don't practice stoicism strictly, you can still profit from it. To situations you find upsetting, you can apply the stoics' logical, sensible, and rational wisdom in the same way you would apply a bandage to a wound. As you do this consistently and frequently, your responses to life's events start to alter. Stoicism eventually becomes second nature to you; it serves as your carry-around first aid kit for philosophical emergencies. This first chapter aims to teach you how to begin applying stoicism in your daily life.

The philosophy holds that the secret to living a good and happy life is to create a great mental attitude, which some stoics connected with being wise and righteous. They believe that if you are in one with nature and have an attitude of apathy toward the outside world, you are living the ideal life. With Zeno, philosophy was born in Greece around 300 BC. Stoicism got its name because Zeno of Citium taught in an Athens location that had a Painted Stoa.

Stoicism is an ancient philosophy that can be interpreted in a variety of ways. From Zeno through Marcus Aurelius, the philosophy evolved over a period of more than five centuries. One of the more common approaches to philosophy is through Epictetus and his renowned three disciplines of desire, action, and assent. We will examine his viewpoints on life and how we interact with it, including how to manage stress and dissatisfaction. Then, at the conclusion of the chapter, we will put his principles to use in contemporary life to give you a fundamental understanding of Stoic philosophy.

Meet Epictetus

Around 55 AD, Epictetus was born a slave in Hierapolis, which is now Pamukkale in Turkey. When I first encountered his teachings, I was a single student who had just arrived at college and was juggling a problematic long-distance relationship. Politics had left me jaded and disillusioned. I had a strong victim mentality. I felt like a burden had been lifted after reading the opening line of Epictetus' The Enchiridion. Some things are under our control, while others are not, he writes at the beginning of the book. According to him, our perception of good and wrong is the one thing we have complete control over and the only thing we should care about if we must.

According to Epictetus, if you pursue reputation, sex, health, or wealth, you will unavoidably experience unhappiness. Anyone who wants to escape being alone, unnoticed, sickly, or poor will experience perpetual irritation and anxiety. He doesn't make the false claim that you can be free of want or fear. They cannot be avoided. Everyone experiences those brief human feelings of anxiety or eagerness. Stoicism involves questioning your flashes to determine if they relate to the things you cannot change. If they do, you ought to respond, "That is not my concern."

Consider your life and your worries. As I discovered, the majority of your sorrow comes not from true loneliness, illness, or trouble but from the guilt you feel believing it might have been prevented. Is it your fault, for instance, that your job is demanding? Where does your shame come from?

Epictetus was owned by a guy by the name of Epaphroditus. He was given permission by his master to pursue liberal studies, and it was via these that he came across Musonius Rufus, a stoic who would later serve as both his mentor and instructor.

Later, when he had earned his freedom, he started to teach philosophy. Even though the political atmosphere at the time caused his life to alter, he continued teaching philosophy until his death. The thing that kept him going was his firm grasp on the boundaries of his power.

Someone paid a high price for his earthenware lamp when he passed away. He allegedly kept his lamp close to his household deities. He learned an important lesson from the lamp that had once been stolen. He discovered from the theft that a man only loses what he already has. This knowledge served as his life's compass.

It is appropriate that the man's job now offers a framework for dealing with difficulties in life because he was born with a handicapped leg that was likely damaged by his master while he was a slave. Epictetus believed that illness only affects your physical well-being, not your capacity for decision-making.

EPICTETUS IN THE WORLD TODAY

Remind yourself that the hurdle will only stand in your way if you allow it if you find yourself in a tight spot, whether it is due to illness or a challenge to your plans.

Remind yourself of your controllable factors: desire

Epictetus begins The Enchiridion with a dictum that has grown to be a cornerstone of stoic philosophy. What do you have in your control, he asks? Epictetus believed that it was honorable to seek only things that you could control. Don't let anything, whether they be outside events or other people, that you cannot control make you angry or upset. Instead, concentrate on your actions. You can let go and accept things as they are with this mindset. It will also give you more power to exert what you can control. We have control over our beliefs, dislikes, desires, and deeds, the man added. We are powerless over our possessions, names, bodies, or the behavior of others.

Establish a standard- Action

It is a universal truth that influential people and true leaders, from all walks of life, hardly ever discuss how things ought to be done. Their behavior demonstrates this. Consider a person you admire. How much did they teach you, and how much did you take away from their decisions? Focus on your daily activities and decisions if you want to be a stoic like Epictetus. Instead of talking about your standards, live them out.

You will use your time and energy most effectively there. Never settle for theorems that do not control your life, just like Epictetus.

Give yourself a character to play – Assent

Epictetus was aware that habit often dictates our behavior and that we have a tendency to believe that habits cannot be changed. He pushed his students to establish standards and guiding concepts for their daily lives. For anyone starting their contact with stoicism, this is a wise move. Do not expect it to be simple, but prescribing a character for yourself and taking baby steps each day in that direction will help you become more of who you want to be. In relation to this book, that character is a resolve to rely on time-tested stoic wisdom during trying times.

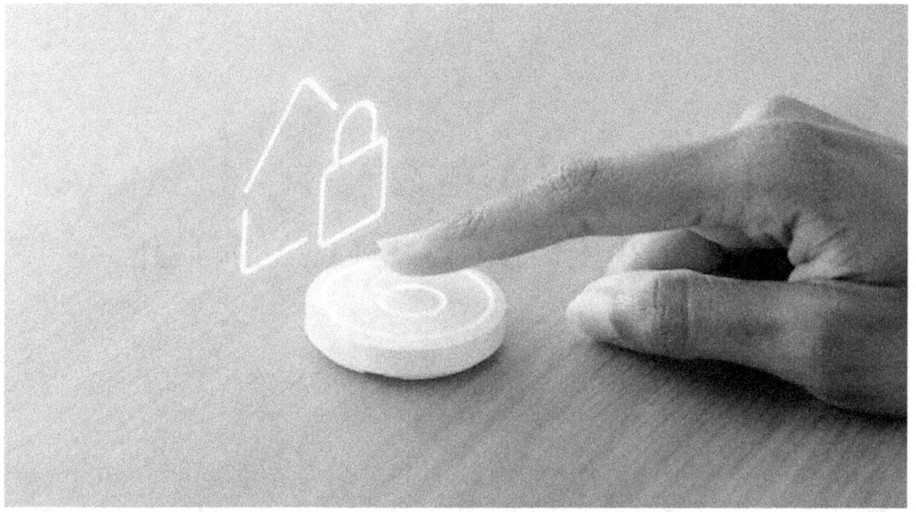

What can you control?

You can start the process of incorporating stoicism into your life by following the three stages in this chapter. You can begin allowing the grapevine to grow and produce fruit. So far, it has become clear that:

Uncontrollable events in life are an inevitable part of life.

If you solely concentrate on the things you can control, you'll be most productive.

Your moral compass and character will direct you in the correct direction.

To help you better comprehend what you are agreeing to, we will discuss the three pillars of stoicism in more detail in the following chapter.

THE THREE PILLARS OF STOICISM ARE EXPLAINED - PURSUE VIRTUE

'Oh, ye who have learned the doctrines of the Stoa, and committed to your divine books, the best human learning, teaching men that virtue is only good! She is the only one who keeps the lives and cities of men safer than walls and gates. Those who place their happiness in pleasure, are led by the least worthy muse.' – Athenaeus the Epigrammatist as quoted by Diogenes.

The majority of the time, when people discuss stoicism, they discuss life's practical rules, which is fine. What use is theory if you can't put it into practice? That is why I wrote this book with that format in mind. But for Zeno the Citium, the philosopher's creator, the question wasn't just about how to live. He organized philosophy into three categories, which became known as the pillars of stoicism—ethics, physics, and logic—because he believed that you might understand life by looking at other profoundly philosophical issues.

He believed that physics dealt with the nature of the cosmos and the universe. When Zeno and the Stoics spoke of physics, they meant the study of the natural and supernatural worlds since they thought the universe to be a divine being. With regard to logos, the second pillar. For him, logic is the way that we as a community and as individuals think about the world. It covers subjects like grammar, rhetoric, perception, and other related fields.

The stoics held that logic is a sort of fire that underlies the universe and that reason is what holds the world together. They contended that since logic must be a component of the material nature of the world, the cosmos can be thought of as divine. According to the Stoics, God was the imaginative and productive force behind the cosmos' creation.

The last pillar includes ethical considerations and practical life-related issues. This is the section that we frequently discuss. This book aims to be practical in every chapter, but I haven't ignored stoicism's physics and logos in the process. Stoic philosophy advocates living in harmony with nature and adjusting your expectations so that you don't go against them. It lives in harmony with the natural world. Let's first examine the three pillars in detail before applying them to your life:

Recognizing Logic

We typically take our capacity for rational thought for granted. Despite the fact that the human mind does not operate in accordance with the cause-and-effect law, we continue to ignore it. Then there is the wide range of individuals who are solely controlled by their emotions. Stoics rejected the idea of letting emotions rule one's actions. Instead, they submitted to reason. They regarded logic as a type of art. No wonder they put a lot of effort into developing their minds. When describing stoic reasoning, Diogenes said: "The sensible man must constantly adore dialect. Arguments make everything clear once it has been thought through. You learn what belongs to the ethos and what belongs to physics through argument.

Consider logic as the sturdy covering that protects physics and morality. To enjoy and gain from the other components of stoicism, you must first learn the steady and reliable technique of logic.

The concept is founded on a few linguistic conventions. For instance, if you are indoors during the day and peek out the window, you will see that it is light outside. It is light, and you can state that with assurance. Your conclusion is accurate if it is indeed daylight; however, if it is nighttime, it is incorrect. The stoics believed that such laws regulate all of reality. Their logos are created. They are universal laws of nature.

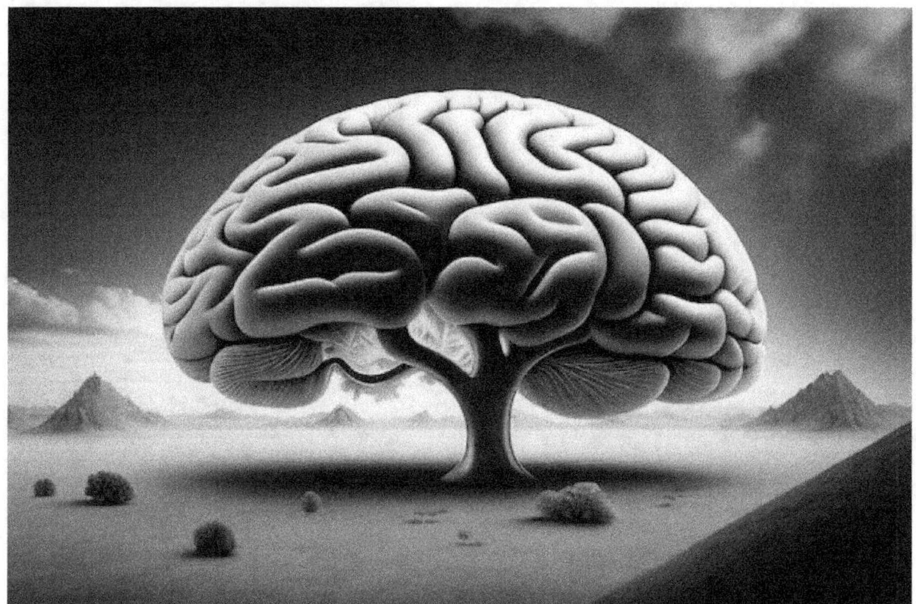

Examining Ethics

The difference between what is appropriate to do and what is not is at the heart of ethics. The stoics contend that once you have mastered logos, you can move on to learning ethics. Virtue and vice were used to divide ethics. Your happiness will always be boosted by virtue, whereas unhappiness is always the byproduct of vice. They continued by classifying virtue and vice according to other divisions, which we will cover later in this book. However, there is a wide range of morally neutral situations between virtue and vice when things are neither good nor terrible.

Things that are ethically neutral are referred to as indifferent by the Stoics. You can act in this gray area, and whether it is moral or immoral will depend on the circumstances. You are able to establish that distinction and choose how to move forward with the aid of your reasoning skills. In essence, indifferent people won't hurt you or make you happier. How you use them will determine how happy you are. How do you utilize them, though? According to Zeno, the goal of life is to proceed without incident along the natural stream of events.

He regarded everything as a component of the system he named "nature." That nature is compatible with a good life.

When your actions are in harmony with nature, you are acting with virtue.Contrarily, vice is when your actions are at odds with nature.

The Stoics distinguished between dispreferred and preferred indifference when it came to indifference. Examples of favored indifference include power, pleasure, and riches. They improve our current state of affairs naturally, but happiness is not a given. Things like poverty, ugliness, frailty, and disease are considered disfavored and indifferent. They slightly exacerbate our preexisting conditions, but they can only make life miserable if you allow them. What determines whether or not you live a happy life depends on how you employ either of the indifferent.

The foundation is physics.

If you do not comprehend nature, you cannot live in harmony with it. The stoics meant nature when they spoke of physics. It shouldn't be mistaken with current physics, as we know it. The goal of stoic physics is to comprehend the cosmos. I will simply cover the fundamentals of the Stoics' extremely sophisticated conception of the universe. They had faith in a supernatural being they termed the logos, or the power of reason. They assert that there are two planes of existence for us: pneuma and matter. Everything that we can sense with our five senses is matter. It is passive, destructible, and lifeless.

The active force that moves the cosmos is pneuma. Despite being completely intertwined with the material world, it is unbreakable. Some Stoics considered the pneuma to be the means through which the logos travel. It is what gives the universe life. It drives the motion of the planets and stars, the sea's waves, and even the existence of life. The stoics believed that everything in life was predetermined. They believed that there are numerous realities and that each one is predetermined. You act out the reality that follows your decisions. This means that your journey is determined by the decisions you make.

It makes sense if this sounds extremely complex. The interaction of the three pillars of stoicism was compared by some scholars to the shape of an egg. Physics is represented by the yolk, ethics by the white, and logic by the shell of the egg. According to these academics, physics motivates stoicism. They contend that you cannot judge what is good or terrible if you do not understand how the universe functions. These pillars are more intertwined than I initially thought. The entire system will fail without one.

ARE YOU PERSUING VIRUE?

Stoics believe that happiness cannot exist without virtue. The stoics believed that pursuing virtue or living in accordance with nature, is the only thing truly good about life. What kind of life are you leading? Do you intentionally or unintentionally pursue vice with the expectation of happiness?

Since the Stoics held the view that nature is divine and that therefore living in accordance with nature is living in accordance with the divine, they connected the pursuit of virtue with happiness. Decide to prioritize pursuing morality over other things.

You need discipline to accomplish this. Discipline is the fundamental behavior, way of thinking, and attitude that will keep you moving forward in your goals. It is what keeps the stoic philosophical framework alive. It will be covered in Chapter 3. Let's review what we've learned for the time being:

- A philosophy known as stoicism is based on the principles of logic, physics, and ethics. The system crumbles in the absence of anyone.
- We think about the universe logically. The practical way we live is called ethics, and it is based on the divine. The world of physics is a divine one.
- Being virtuous will make you happy.

MARCUS AURELIUS AND SELF-DISCIPLINE - DISCIPLINE IS FREEDOM

'You could be good today, but instead, you are choosing tomorrow.' – Marcus Aurelius.

We currently live in a time when many individuals experience anxiety, dread, and doubt. Everyone is constantly wondering, "How do I find the strength to keep going?" How am I to make sense of life? Does adversity improve you?

Even though life never actually stops moving, difficult moments might make you feel as though everything is lost. What should you do in that case?

Can you recover after a crisis? That question would receive a hearty "yes" from the stoics. If you approach a crisis with the appropriate attitude, you can emerge stronger. You can learn from it how to forgive, grow stronger, let go of the past, and other life lessons. yet why do the majority of individuals experience crises yet never grow?

It turns out that self-discipline is something that many individuals lack, and that without it, no personal success, goal, or achievement can be attained. They start whatever they are doing without the commitment to finish it. When a crisis arises, they inevitably move on to the next task just to repeat the cycle. The most crucial quality you need to achieve any level of brilliance is self-discipline. It is what you require to continue in your pursuit of virtue, as we stated in the last chapter. Of all the stoic philosophies, it is the most useful. This chapter will examine what discipline is, what hinders it, and how to develop it using the lessons Marcus Aurelius taught us.

What is self-control?

Self-discipline is the capacity to push oneself and maintain a path of action despite negative feelings, according to its definition. The majority of people desire it, yet its development is becoming more challenging. It's understandable why people are worried about forming healthy habits given the growing number of months designated for it — No Nut November, Stoptober, DryJanuary, you name it! In these months, groups of individuals come together to encourage self-control and abstinence from vices like drinking and porn. These are excellent suggestions since they show a readiness to develop constructive habits. But it's not particularly simple to change habits, as the majority of people inevitably discover.

How many times have you set objectives or made plans, telling yourself that you would act differently this time, only to give up after a few days? How often have you given in to your whims and gone back to your routines? It takes discipline to resist your immediate desires. You need discipline to achieve your goals, whether they be to grow your business, spend more time with your family, or reduce your weight. You must resist the urge to snack, watch mindless television, or engage in other time-wasting activities.

I'm not arguing that if you practice discipline, the temptation won't still be there. For instance, you'll want to take it easy. The capacity to withstand that emotion is self-discipline. You become more disciplined the more you push back against it. This is so because willpower is a muscle. I must emphasize that motivation and discipline are not the same thing. You can get things done with the help of motivation, but it comes and goes. You will postpone or revert to your old behaviors if you only rely on motivation. Consistency in the discipline. Even when you lack motivation, it aids in movement. Self-control is freedom.

WHY IS IT DIFFICULT TO GET DISCIPLINED?

It's difficult to discipline yourself. It is comparable to climbing a mountain without a peak while trekking. Developing discipline is made considerably more challenging by two factors:

Temptation

It is more difficult to control our impulses because there are so many distractions and sources of temptation all around us. YouTube, video games, and social media come to mind as examples of things that compete for our attention and keep us hooked. Self-discipline is more difficult to attain because of all the noise, but it shouldn't be an excuse.

Without Resistance

There are fewer opportunities to be disciplined the easier your life is. Discipline deteriorates when things are easy, and today's world is all about ease. Just take a glance around you: Amazon offers quick next-day delivery; you can order meals and have them in 30 minutes; social media provides dopamine doses whenever you want them; Netflix allows you to view anything you want, anytime. The list continues. Instant pleasure is taking away chances to practice self-control. We are becoming hurried, forgetful people as a result of it.

Unfortunately, as the world of commerce and retail moves toward providing us with convenience, it also eliminates our sources of resistance.

For discipline to develop, resistance is necessary. Comfort in excess can be a trap. Your discipline may be being hampered by too much comfort. You require opposition. The catalyst for growth is it. It empowers you to expand beyond your current abilities and restrictions by revealing them to you. What then should we do? How can one develop self-control?

HOW TO IMPROVE YOUR SELF-CONTROL WITH MARCUS AURELIUS

The majority of the time, our ego will urge us to flee any discomfort or resistance. This always occurs at the start of each new endeavor. that is normal to anticipate that as you begin to use stoic wisdom. Thankfully, the stoics didn't remain mute on this subject. Marcus Aurelius is credited as having the most to say about self-control, which is the foundation of stoicism. He formerly held a position that was among the most powerful in the entire globe. He had the option to get anything he wanted. The following observations about developing self-discipline can be found in his book "Meditations," in which he found time to write during his rule.

Discover your mission

Marcus Aurelius held the view that every person has a function or something for which they were made. He preached that it is our moral obligation to identify and fulfill that purpose. You will be motivated to get up every morning and take the necessary action if you have a purpose. You are more likely to finish every daily activity if you have a clear understanding of your goals and how everything you do helps you achieve them.

Knowing you're why is the most important source of self-discipline. Once you understand why, even if you are unsure of how to go, all you need to do is begin. Just write something every day if you want to be an author. Do it because it's what you're supposed to do. You advance because of the internal motivation provided by your mission. Finding a strong motivation to continue doing something is the essence of self-discipline.

Believe in yourself

Make your passion a rock, as Marcus Aurelius once advised. Feed your cravings and keep your attention on yourself. The next step after determining your purpose is to create a workable action plan to help you achieve your objective. Don't simply commit to the big picture; also commit to the smaller steps that will help you get there. No of the difficulties, make a commitment to doing whatever is necessary. No matter how you're feeling or how you're feeling mentally or physically, self-control keeps you on track.

Every aspect of your life, including the things you desire to be, do, and have, depends on your capacity to take the necessary steps to realize your objectives, whether or not you are motivated to do so.

Make careful to base your action plan's development on manageable daily goals as you establish them. You feel more in control of your actions as a result. It aids in keeping you from experiencing stress. Being overburdened can lead to procrastination, which eventually causes you to veer off course or become stuck. You can't reasonably claim to be self-disciplined when that occurs.

Show up every day.

Marcus Aurelius believed that every life is constructed from many life deeds. If a daily action accomplishes the best goal it possibly could on that particular day, you must be happy with it. It works like this: even after discovering your purpose and creating a solid plan, you may still struggle with maintaining discipline. It is possible to lack consistency. The key to consistency is being present every day.

Come in and do the work. The more times you participate, the simpler it will be to participate again. Consistency is the habit of self-discipline. Remind yourself each morning that a new day means a fresh start to your life. Focus on the area in front of you.

Voluntarily subject oneself to suffering

Marcus Aurelius observed that "we should practice discipline in the small matters and then move on to bigger things" in one of his notebook entries. It will be more beneficial to accept his advice and willingly put yourself through difficulty in the modern world where convenience reigns supreme. Making your life a little uncomfortable as part of your routine is what voluntary hardship is all about. In this manner, you prepare yourself to be truly tough on the day that you need to be. Anything from taking cold showers to giving up smoking might be considered a voluntary hardship. You will begin to realize that you can live without some of these conveniences as you subject yourself to these challenges.

Don't make yourself a victim.

Marcus was a strong supporter of taking action without complaining. You become a victim if you claim things like "I was born this way" or "I was never taught anything else." They serve as justifications for continuing in your current course rather than improving. They result from a victim attitude that asks "Why me?" absolving you of responsibility and undermining self-control. Develop the ability to view situations from a position of strength rather than self-pity. Never shift responsibility when anything goes wrong. You must be a person of action who doesn't give up control or avoid responsibilities if you want to practice self-discipline.

Postpone gratification

According to Marcus Aurelius, humans should contribute to maintaining order in the same way that birds, ants, and bees do.

The Stoics believed that people were not simply born to feel well. Doing what nature requires is admirable, and you cannot accomplish that without postponing gratification. Experiencing delayed gratification involves delaying your desired outcome. It involves putting off what you desire now in order to acquire something better later on. It involves avoiding temptation while you stay committed to your goals.

Ignore the naysayers.

Don't spend more time on insignificant things than necessary. Marcus Aurelius had something to say about doubters. When other people accuse, despise, or condemn you, it says more about who they are than about you.

You will understand that you don't need to worry about what people think of you once you accept this reality. If you begin pursuing your purpose and making the necessary efforts to realize it, it is inevitable. Those who criticize usually do so out of a sense of humiliation or dread about their own apparent lack of self-control. Trying to talk to them is a waste of time. Give them no more of your time. Use the advice of those you respect instead, and disregard all other opinions.

Examine your days.

The intelligent soul is conscious of itself. It grows when one examines oneself and when one makes one's own decisions. It is successful in achieving its goal. Studying oneself and being aware of one's blind spots, in the words of Marcus Aurelius, is one of the most important strategies to develop self-discipline. While doing this, be brutally honest. Make it a practice to actively learn more about who you are each night while you reflect. Then, create solutions to your weaknesses. Every day, ask yourself, "What went well?" "Where was my discipline put to the test?" What can I do to improve? After you've provided your answers to these questions, do not berate yourself. Apologize to yourself and make a commitment to improve tomorrow.

HOW SELF-DISCIPLINED ARE YOU?

Marcus Aurelius viewed stoicism as a comforting remedy for a wound rather than as a lofty, stern teacher. Epictetus accurately characterized life as harsh, constrained, punitive, and stifling. We receive the assistance we require from stoicism to make the most of such a life. We have established in this chapter that:

- Self-discipline is about controlling our urges.
- If there is resistance, it can grow like a muscle.
- Marcus Aurelius offered a road plan for developing self-control, which includes practices like postponing gratification, shunning doubters, and showing up every day.

How can we apply stoicism to our lives in order to make them flourish? is the question we consider in the following chapter. We will examine Epictetus' life metaphors and draw guidance from them in order to discover how to have a contented and moral life.

EPICTETUS' DETAILED INSTRUCTION FOR LIFE – ATTITUDE MATTERS

'How long will you wait before you demand the best for yourself?' – Epictetus.

It has been mentioned again that how we approach life counts. Our mindset determines how we behave. The appropriate mindset helps us achieve success. If you have the incorrect mindset, all the handshakes and grins in the world won't help. However, there hasn't been much stated about what the correct attitude is or how to acquire it. How do you deal with anything life throws at you and what is the finest life you can lead? What makes you thrive? The solution is a stoic outlook. It's about realizing that what other people do is neither your concern nor your obligation. We are all accountable for the daily thoughts and deeds we commit.

Metaphors for life: Epictetus

Epictetus used a few analogies from life to describe that way of thinking. Here, we'll look at some of Epictetus' metaphors to help you understand and internalize the stoic philosophy of life.

Life is a celebration.

Epictetus viewed life as a celebration that God had planned for us. This perspective on life makes things seem enjoyable. You have your eye firmly fixed on the bigger picture, and you are equipped to handle any challenges that come your way. You are aware of the important play in which you are participating. Epictetus invites you to determine your role as one of the festival participants. Did not God, the mastermind behind the festival, bring you here? What was his motivation? He did not create you as a mortal. Epictetus said that you should make use of your mortality and the brief period of time you have left on earth. Why not take advantage of the opportunity to briefly engage with God in his festival and pageant?

Stoic ethics is all about taking part in the celebration while also doing your part to make God's beautiful city a better place to live and work.

Life is a game.

We should be like dice players, Epictetus advised in Discourses of Epictetus as he urged his students to embrace and accept the idea that some things outside of ourselves are immoral. Neither the counter nor the dice have any actual value in a dice game. The way you approach the game is what counts and can make a difference. That is how the stoic outlook sees the world. Epictetus also uses the experience of playing a game of baseball as an illustration. Nobody considers the ball to be a terrible or good thing while the players are rushing and squabbling for it at that precise moment. The players' ability to catch or throw the ball with the necessary expertise is the only thing that matters. What counts are the players' quickness, good judgment, and dexterity? If a person uses their abilities and skill effectively, they have performed well.

In other passages of his writing, Epictetus compares suicide to video games. When a player no longer finds the game enjoyable, they stop playing. He believed that was how things should be in life. No, he was proposing that people stop living when life becomes intolerable rather than calling for suicide. His argument was that if you view life as a game, then it is time for you to enter the arena and participate. You cannot afford to watch from the sidelines and criticize players as if you will be given the chance to take their place. You have the responsibility to take up position and toss the ball.

Life is like weaving.

Epictetus linked this metaphor to the idea that life is like a game. Wool is used by the weaver to create cloth when weaving. In the game metaphor, the wool serves the same purpose as the ball. It is our responsibility to make the best textile we can out of wool and to use it as intended.

Life is a play

In a previous chapter, we talked about how developing self-discipline is aided by discovering our purpose. It aids in bringing to mind who we are and our purpose for existing. The 'here' in that statement is the subject of this metaphor. It offers the idea of embracing one's fate, whatever it may be, and sees life as a performance. The part we play in the play of life is not our choice. We want to play a particular character, but we must recognize that getting that position is fate. When you consider living in this way, you always keep in mind that you are a play's performer, not the play's author. Whether or not that play is short or long will be decided by God. You will play the cripple if that is what he wants you to do. Make sure you do a good job if he asks you to play the role of the poor man, a private individual, or a government employee. You must perform admirably in the function that has been assigned to you.

Life is a competition.

You can draw a parallel between someone's physical preparation for competing in the arena and your training in stoic ethics as preparation for flourishing in life in this metaphor. Epictetus was addressing those who were upset that they did not have enough time to study as much as they would like to or to prepare for their upcoming tasks as they would have liked to. If you decide to study, you should consider it a preparation for life, which consists of more than just books. Think of a player entering a field to play. He makes his way to the stadium's middle before sobbing openly. When questioned, he claims that the reason he is sobbing is that he is inside the stadium instead of exercising outside. See how ridiculous that is? But how often do you put off completing something because you lack the necessary skills?

The crying athlete in the story overlooks the fact that they were training for the stadium. That point is reached after much weight pumping and rock climbing. Are you still struggling to lift weights when it's time to take action? It's like being faced with a decision and instead of making it, asking to read a treatise on the subject. It's similar to practicing for an athletic event to read this book and perform other activities that get you ready to pursue the stoic ideal. Although the training is occasionally unpleasant, challenging, and demanding, it prepares you for the real world. When you consider life to be a competition, you must consider moving forward. When facing a challenge, keep in mind that the Olympics are currently in progress and that the contest is currently underway. The game can no longer be postponed.

Military service is life.

The stoics thought that God controls the cosmos. They held the view that everyone serves God, whether they like it or not. The lesson Epictetus was trying to convey to his students through this metaphor was that they should conduct their lives in an effort to carry out their military service to the highest standards. This metaphor is for you if you're frustrated by everything you have to do. It serves as a reminder to live your life as a soldier called to duty. While there, one guy must keep watch, another must take the field, and a third must conduct reconnaissance. They cannot all stay in the camp. If they did, no one would receive service.

The key takeaway from this is to always follow through on your commitments. You are unable to complain to the general again. Being a serving soldier and choosing to complain constantly overdoing your duty is a pitiful thing. Everyone would stop acting; no soldier would build a barrier, dig trenches, or engage in field combat if everyone did that. The world is also like that. Our entire lives are campaigns. To fulfill the general's orders, it is up to you to be the finest soldier you can be. You must whenever possible ascertain the general's desires and carry them out.

How do you view your life?

What mindset do you bring to every situation? Are you failing to have fun, contribute, or toss the ball? This chapter has demonstrated that life is a celebration;

- Take pleasure in it.
- The game of life. Make good use of your tools; it's weaving.

- Be a good actor; life is a play.
- Athletic competition is a life. Participate.
- Live like a soldier and fulfill your obligations.

We will examine the stoics' views on virtue in the following chapter. Since pursuing virtue is a prerequisite for pleasure, how do you achieve it and what do we mean by virtue?

STOIC VIRTUE EXPLAINED - THE HIGHEST GOOD

'If it is not right, do not do it. If it is not true, do not say it.' – Marcus Aurelius.

Cicero, probably Rome's finest orator, created the phrase "the highest good." The thing we should be pursuing in life is referred to as the highest good. As I said earlier, virtue is the highest good in the eyes of the Stoics. The Stoics believed that every challenge we meet in life, whatever its form, presents an opportunity for a noble reaction. Situations can be frightening and distressing, but you must respond with virtue. They continued by saying that if you act morally, happiness, reputation, success, love, and honor all follow. The guy of morality will then have everything they require to live happily. However, what exactly did the Stoics intend by virtue? We will enlarge on their definition of virtue and discuss how to apply it to our own lives in this chapter. The four virtues that the stoics held in high regard were wisdom, temperance, courage, and justice.

PERCEIVING STOCKS VIRTUE

Wisdom

The essential purpose of life, in Epictetus' view, is to know and distinguish between different things so that you can see yourself clearly and understand what you can and cannot control. He continued by saying that virtue and evil are found within, not in the uncontrollable outside world. We choose between good and evil. Knowing this entails knowledge of wisdom and virtue. According to Diogenes, the stoics defined knowledge as the capacity to distinguish between what is good and evil and what is neither good nor evil. It involves being aware of what to choose, what to avoid, and what to disregard. Once you are aware of this, your behavior alters.

Between response and stimulus, there is a gap where the capacity to choose is located, as Viktor Frankl is quoted as having said. Wisdom has a chance to shine in that environment. Recognizing that space is the first step toward increasing wisdom. It's where you put the teachings you've studied into practice or ignore them, leading to unreasonable and impulsive behavior. Seneca defined wisdom as the capacity to harness philosophy and apply it to everyday life.

Temperance

Marcus Aurelius discussed calmly in his book Meditations, contending that if you wish to be at peace with yourself and your life, do only what is required or less. Living in peace entails merely acting as a social person when necessary. It is to get rid of unnecessary things. He advised his students to always ask themselves, "Is this necessary?"

The identical concept was discussed by Aristotle, however, he referred to it as the "golden mean." He continued by saying that goodness might be found between excess and insufficiency. Excess is a representation of discontent and dissatisfaction. Living beyond one's means is to yield to a self-defeating impulse.

Epictetus advised people in his books to "restrain your desire" and "do not let your heart follow many things" in order to obtain what they needed. Seneca reasoned along similar lines. He advised keeping your money to a minimum and only having what is required and sufficient. Knowing you have plenty when you have what you need is the definition of temperance. The stoics frequently discussed exercising self-control in the face of pleasure, success, financial possessions, and even adulation and agony. To be temperate, one must guard against extremes so that they do not depend on pleasure for happiness or permit pain's impermanence to sabotage enjoyment.

Courage

According to Epictetus, if life is like military duty, you must contribute to the flow of events. You must acknowledge that you are engaged in a complex and protracted war. The key to winning the battle is your station, and you remain there for the rest of your days. When Epictetus was questioned about this viewpoint, he responded that in order for individuals to flourish, they must be prepared to struggle and persevere. A perennially relevant symbol of stoic philosophy is courage. It is represented by a lone knight who continues to battle in a conflict he will never possibly win. Publius Clodius showed courage by taking against Nero in a contest that would endanger his life.

Marcus Aurelius is depicted as refusing to be corrupted by power and choosing to uphold morality despite the fact that Rome was in decline.

The great southern stoics display courage by choosing bravery generation after generation. LeRoy made the decision to take up the Klan. It is Walker Percy rejecting the bigotry that was prevalent in his time and choosing to be a light of goodness, and it is William Alexander adopting his cousins. It is Publius Rufus defending himself and bringing about change. The last words of Seneca were, "He may kill me, but he does me no harm." Even though they were ultimately pointless, each of these battles required a lot of bravery. They demanded a commitment to challenging the existing quo.

When Publius Clodius spoke candidly about Nero, he put himself on the line. He lost as a result. When the Percys fought for the rights of others, they put their reputation and safety in danger. Marcus Aurelius posed a threat to his authority. The stoics regard that as bravery. It takes courage to accept bad luck and put one's life in danger for a fellow human. It is the resolve to uphold your values even when it is uncomfortable. It involves expressing your truth and acting in accordance with your convictions.

Justice

According to Marcus Aurelius, we are obligated by birth to pursue fairness in all of our dealings. Every righteous deed serves the greater good. Marcus Aurelius considered justice to be the most important of the four stoic virtues. How impressive is selfish courage, in his view, since fairness is the mother of all virtues? What use is wisdom if it is solely used for one's own benefit? Cicero, who shared ideas with Marcus Aurelius, must be taken into consideration in order to comprehend justice as a virtue. Justice, in his opinion, is the pinnacle of all other qualities. Cicero not only preached about "the highest good," but also acted accordingly. Despite being a senator in Rome and taking on a significant position at a young age, Cicero did not always view justice in the same way that we do now.

Justice was broad to men like Cicero and the Stoics. It covers our responsibility to and relationships with others. It is the guiding concept that controls how society functions and keeps a group together. According to this theory, no one has the right to injure another person, no one has a claim to another person's private property, and we are created with the intention of serving others. It also embraces the notion that nature inspires people to be kind to one another. It represents constancy, accuracy, and good faith. Any action that causes harm to another person is considered unjust.

The radical aspect of stoic philosophy is arguably the virtue of fairness.

The idea that everything in the world is interconnected is based on this. We are all connected, and, in the words of Marcus Aurelius, "what harms the hive, harms the bee." We are all connected, therefore if you injure someone else, you hurt yourself. Epictetus elaborated, noting that having high standards for oneself is equivalent to actively caring for others. If that's the case, which it is, then the most noble thing a guy can do is uphold equality and act in humanity's best interests.

Are you enjoying yourself?

You need virtue if you want to be free and happy in life. Thankfully, virtue is not nebulous or lofty. Complex concepts that required complicated applications did not appeal to the stoics. A stoic holds that they can only control how they respond to the world, and that reaction should be done with courage, justice, wisdom, and temperance. In fact, if I had to sum up virtue as the Stoics understood it in one sentence, I would say this. Life has no set pattern. There are many things outside of your control. You can feel paralyzed and overwhelmed by that concept, or you might feel liberated. This chapter has demonstrated that virtue is what makes the realization of the things outside of your control liberating.

If you are moral, you are aware that you can use logic to weigh your options no matter what happens. You are aware that you will make an effort to act morally and virtuously.

Lucius, often known as Seneca, was a Roman senator and stoic philosopher who ascended to become one of the most important individuals in the Roman Empire. His life had both highs and lows, as is typical of human existence. The man experienced grief, suffering, conflict, and drama. Seneca was appointed Nero's closest advisor after the Roman Empire was established in AD 54. At the moment, his life was going extremely well. Their intimate friendship collapsed a few years later. Seneca was thus told by the emperor to end his life since he was allegedly involved in an aborted assassination attempt on Nero. He was most likely innocent. But despite the prospect of death, he persisted in his stoic views. He reportedly maintained his composure when the suicide protocol was put into motion.

Veins had to be cut off according to ancient Roman suicide practice so that you may bleed to death. You have to consume poison as well. Seneca experienced that. We still discuss him and draw heavily from his writings more than 2000 years later. He spoke about a variety of topics, like relationships, mortality, riches, and happiness, but in this section, we'll focus on his views on making the most of your time.

Examine your daily routine.

It is typical to hear individuals lament the passing of time. This notion was rejected by Seneca's ideas. If you approach your time as your most valuable resource, you have all the time you need to lead an outstanding life, he contended. Most of the time, individuals are thrifty with their money and possessions, yet they waste their time carelessly as if it were worthless. Keep in mind that while you can get back lost money, you can never get back lost time.

Time is only limited if it is wasted, according to a saying by Seneca. He accepted that time is limited, but he contended that our wastefulness made it even shorter. He argued that the reason our lives are short is not because we live ungratefully. If we make wise use of our time, we have a long enough life and plenty of time to pursue our best aspirations. Seneca continued by saying that if you know how to live, life is lengthy. How do you spend your time then?

Finding out how you spend your time is the first step in improving your time management. To keep track of what you accomplish each day, you can try keeping a daily journal for a week. This kind of audit will show you where you waste time, what goals are achievable for the day, and where you should put your energy. You will begin to realize how much time you waste on useless conversations, thoughts, and actions as you go through this audit. The amount of time you require for particular jobs will become more apparent to you. You will also be able to determine the time of day when you are most productive.

Establish a schedule and include incentives.

Going about their days without a plan is one of the blunders people make when trying to better manage their time. Every day must have a timetable before it can start. Make it a routine to make a to-do list every morning. Alternatively, write a list of everything you need to get done and give each item a day at the start of each week. You won't need to fret about all the things you haven't done at night if your plans are written down. Additionally, when you prepare ahead, your subconscious will begin digesting your ideas while you are sleeping, allowing you to wake up the next morning with new perspectives. Making a detailed plan will help you avoid wasting time by not hopping between jobs.

Both the stoics and I do not guarantee that this will be easy. Create an immediate incentive for your goals as Seneca adds another step to this concept that might help you stay on track with your plan. Research has shown that the ongoing conflict between short-term gain and long-term objectives, or "present bias," is one of the reasons we put off doing things. This bias, according to Seneca, is the worst hindrance to life. Your brain creates mental images of your past, present, and future selves.

Every time you set a goal for a better future, you are preparing for a future version of yourself that values discipline and long-term rewards. However, when you have to take action, your present self battles your future self and typically prevails.

Seneca's solution to this issue is to make the incentives for achieving your objectives immediate. For instance, join a gym or a team sport if you want to become someone who exercises frequently but likes to socialize. While pursuing your objective, you will have the opportunity to mingle. It will be simpler to do everything you need to do each day if you are creative with your rewards.

Your workload should be limited.

Setting time constraints for specific jobs rather than completing them as soon as possible should be a big component of your timetable; otherwise, it could feel like you are not moving forward. Try taking a break every hour to balance concentration and rest so that you may avoid mental fatigue and maintain your motivation. When the allotted time for a task is over, move on to the next crucial duty. Your productivity will rise as your list of things to do gets less.

Be careful not to overachieve, though. Seneca asserts that if you relentlessly pursue success and your goals, you will suffer and have a shorter lifespan.

You will achieve your goals if you live that way, but you will have done so anxiously. If you live your life just for success, you have forgotten that time is fleeting. As soon as you accomplish one, a new one is placed in its place. You work for the sake of working until there is no more suffering since ambition breeds ambition. If you still feel that Seneca went too far, think about how consumerist society is today. To obtain more goods, we attempt to work longer and harder. The result? stress, anxiety, anxiety, and burnout. Limiting your tasks can help you stay focused and prevent you from sliding into the consumerism trap.

Reflect on death

Seneca believed that one of the reasons we spend so much of our time is because we fail to remember that no one survives this world. We lose time because we act as though we have infinite time. We seldom consider how vulnerable we are or how much time has passed. We waste time because we think we have plenty of it, despite the fact that the day we spend on something insignificant might be the last one we have. Seneca was right when he said that how we approach death influences how we live. We will take our days for granted and waste time if we believe that death is far away. How often do you consider dying? Has it become firmly entrenched in your heart as inevitable and real?

You can prevent wasting time on pointless planning by practicing death meditation. According to Seneca, we spend the majority of our time planning for the future rather than enjoying the present. He continued by saying that everyone goes through life concerned by the future and worn out by the here and now. He who organizes his today as though it were his final day neither longs for nor fears the next day. You can quit delaying your happiness by thinking about death because you'll realize that the future you're fixated on doesn't actually exist.

Pursue one task at a time.

Avoiding the desire to multitask is one of the simplest methods to enhance your time management abilities. Distractions should be avoided while you concentrate on one work at a time. While multitasking may be alluring, if you give in, you'll be setting yourself up for failure. As you attempt to balance multiple tasks, you will wind up wasting time and being less effective. As a general rule, stay away from the busyness trap. It is the supreme diversion. The general consensus favors being occupied. It announces activity as though it were a virtue. According to Seneca, being busy is a delusion that actually steals your time. Nobody who is busy can pursue anything successfully.

While the truth is that our internal states have a greater impact on our productivity than external factors like social media, emails, and other people, we frequently blame these factors for our troubles maintaining focus. Being busy indicates a bad internal condition. It's just a symptom, really. It is an attempt to avoid being alone and to get away from reality. If you can't sit quietly in a room by yourself, you can't be very productive.

How do you spend your time?

Here is a summary of everything we discovered in this chapter:

- Your most valuable, finite resource is time.
- Behave in that manner.
- Consider dying and live each day as if it were your last.
- Multitasking is a falsehood, and being busy is an illusion.
- Establish a timetable and give yourself rewards for doing tasks.

How are you spending each day now that you've audited your days? Get off the hamster wheel of existence in a world where everything is constantly in motion and savor each day. It might be your final.

5 THINGS THAT DISTURB INNER PEACE

'What upsets people is not things themselves, but their judgments about these things.' – Epictetus.

I stated in the previous chapter that if you can't spend time by yourself in a quiet area, you can't be productive. Most people have never experienced mental clarity. Inner serenity seems like a myth to them since they are so accustomed to a turbulent inner environment. Inner tranquility was important to the stoics. To help you achieve some of that inner calmness, we will discuss how stoics deal with their negative emotions in this chapter of the book. I will address each problematic emotion in a separate chapter, but let's first look at what gets in the way of finding inner peace. In this manner, you will be aware of what you will be trying to get rid of.

A wish to be acknowledged

What other people think of us is one of the things we are powerless over. We can shape how others perceive us, but even if we followed all the appropriate steps, it is ultimately up to them whether to accept us or not. There will be those who will despise you without cause. Life is inherently like that. But for many people, the need for approval still robs them of their peace. To deal with this, you must acknowledge that seeking approval from others is weak because you are unable to do so. Epictetus once observed that pursuing things that are out of your control is not a virtue. You don't have to let other people decide how happy you are.

Concern about the future and regret for the past

If you can't let the past go, your mind will never be at peace. You strain yourself and your luggage continues becoming heavier if you carry events from the past. You are powerless to alter the past, which is the issue. Furthermore, you can't rely on your mind to accurately recount events from the past. Those tales are repeated in our brains, tainted by prejudice. Instead, you should take the insightful lessons from your experience and let the incident pass while retaining the lesson. Remind yourself that everything is temporary.

According to Marcus Aurelius, time is like a river; once something occurs, it is quickly washed away and replaced by another.

When dealing with worry over the past, one must make the decision to flow with time rather than clinging to the past or projecting expectations for the future. Another frequent robber of inner calm is a concern for the future. How calm can you be if your thoughts are anchored in an unrealized future? What good does it do to keep thinking about all the possible "what ifs"? The future is not completely certain. If you don't accept it and always appreciate the results you obtain, it could cause anxiety.

The obsession with perfection

Perfectionists make themselves anxious by aiming for an impossible ideal. They feel restless because their work is insufficient. No single outcome, therefore, fulfills them. They are perpetually unhappy with who they are and what they are able to do. Instead of seeking perfection, go for excellence. Perfection is impossible to achieve, but excellence is.

The dread of dying

The other category consists of persons who are preoccupied with delaying aging and are terrified of dying. Aging and death are unavoidable, as history has demonstrated. While adopting good habits and taking care of your body can help you live longer, aging is ultimately unavoidable. When you refuse to acknowledge that death is inevitable, you put yourself through unnecessary distress.

Aversion to the unknown

Yet another group is still afraid of the unknown. They are afraid of individuals from other cultures because they are unfamiliar or they are afraid of flying if they have never been on an aircraft. Being on guard around novelty is instinctive, but fear of the unknown extends beyond that. It makes you imagine scenarios in your head that rob your calm and your faith in the process of being. These dreams about what might be are what this does to you.

Where is your inner calm?

Whatever it is that makes you feel uneasy creates a story in your head that either makes you feel stressed, anxious, angry, or frustrated. It alters the way reality is perceived and makes you behave irrationally. You wind up devoting time and effort to issues that are beyond your control. Before we examine how the stoics handled these strong feelings, let's review what we have discovered:

- When we allow them to, the fear of the future, the fear of death, the need to be accepted, and other circumstances take our inner calm.
- Anything that disturbs our inner serenity does so by exploiting our incapacity to manage our emotions and internal story.

The world is not within our control. There is no guarantee that the things we fear will not come to pass, but by embracing stoic wisdom, you can ensure for yourself that you will react with a clear head and powerful action.

HOW EPICTETUS KEEPS CALM

'It's not what happens to you, but how you react to it that matters.' – Epictetus.

We encounter annoyances every day. We're required to. There are times when our expectations are not met. We hear unfavorable news. When fate appears to have a different agenda than we do, we become irritated. When our efforts to exert more control are unsuccessful, our faith in their success wanes. Then, after coping with the same problems at the beginning of the cycle, we find ourselves there again. How can we break the cycle? How do we maintain composure in the face of chaos so that we can choose wisely?

Review your concept of the self

Epictetus had a more focused and limited understanding of the "self" than most people do. Most of us consider our status and reputation to be a part of our "self." The same sentiment even applies to our property.

In the end, such items are legally ours. However, it is this perspective that causes us to feel powerless or uncontrollable over what constitutes "us." The viewpoint of Epictetus was totally radical. Although he was always at the whim of his master and never had much property, his sense of identity was unaffected.

He allegedly said to his students, "Even Zeus could not break my will. You can chain my leg." He even occasionally dissociated his will from his body. His body belonged to his master because he was a slave.

We can take a cue from his demeanor. Even while we are free, our bodies are ultimately not ours. If they were, we could use our willpower to cure any disease, including cancer. Some of our freedoms may be restricted by events beyond our control, but not our willpower.

If we realize that our will is entirely within our control, it will never be violated. You won't ever give your peace of mind to anything or anyone other than yourself if you learn this lesson.

Practice your goals.

Epictetus suggests practicing your intentions in advance if you wish to remain composed under pressure. Set a parallel purpose to stay in harmony with nature whenever you perform something where there are many variables outside your control. Make up your mind in advance that you will be sensible no matter what. According to the Stoics, persons are "possessed of reason."

To put it another way, only people have the capacity for reason. Being rational is operating in accordance with nature.

Epictetus demonstrated to his students what it looks like to practice your intentions. Going to public baths was a significant pastime tradition of the period. Every time he planned a visit, he would determine in advance that he would maintain his composure even if his belongings were taken. His goal was to maintain his composure. Do you have an intention? Consider going to a restaurant and discovering that the table you choose has not been cleaned. How would you respond? Would you still enjoy yourself? Imagine asking the waiter to wipe the table but getting no response. Then what? Would you raise a fuss? Understanding that using reason is entirely up to you is the rationale behind setting an intention.

Pause to consider the circumstance

When faced with challenges, Epictetus would ponder, "What is outside of my control?" Understanding how little control we have while riding an emotional wave always comes as a shock. Develop the ability to pause and consider this. It will remove anything that is not within your power to resolve, leaving you with a clear understanding of what is within your "will." You can find solace in the knowledge that all you have control over is how you perceive the world once you realize how little else there is.

Determine your course of action.

You can acquire perspective by pausing, but that perspective will be useless if you continue to behave emotionally.

Decide how you will control it once you have a strong grasp on what you can control. The majority of Epictetus' life was spent as a slave. Slaves were dehumanized and robbed of their identity and dignity back then. His name itself implies "property," yet he was able to shape his fate by choosing how to react to the things that were under his control.

Can you remain composed when under stress?

We are lured by fate to give in to unhappiness, anger, or aggravation as we go about our lives. This chapter has taught us that: It is in our control how we react.

To ensure that we remain composed, we can make our objectives known in advance. In the heat of the moment, pausing is usually beneficial.

CONTROLLING YOUR ANGER LIKE SENECA

'We should not control anger, but destroy it completely. What control is there for something that is fundamentally wicked?' – Seneca.

Eneca suggested several strategies for controlling rage. He frequently referred to fury as momentary insanity. Even when our anger is warranted, he argued, we should never act on it since doing so always has a negative impact on our mental health. Here are five strategies to help you manage your rage like Seneca:

Keep in mind that rage is damaging

Seneca never considered rage to be useful. He believed that anyone who is fully aware of the flaws in anger and its capacity to impair sound judgment will be able to resist being furious. Understanding how destructive anger can be is a crucial first step toward controlling it. The ideas of Aristotle regarding rage are on the other end of the spectrum. Anger isn't always a terrible thing, according to Aristotle. For instance, if you become furious in the appropriate situation and at the appropriate moment, your anger is justified.

According to Aristotle, the secret to success is to maintain a neutral stance. They view patience as a virtue.

With Seneca, there was no discernible level of rage. This is not to imply that he (or other stoics) was complacent in the face of injustice. The stoics have faith in human reason. They held the opinion that all aspects of life should be governed by reason. Anger is the most illogical emotion there is. According to Seneca, anger is unnatural since it transforms you into a slave, cannot be controlled, and spreads easily.

Discover your triggers

If you give it any thought, you'll notice that some situations tend to aggravate you more than others that you come across frequently. Locate them. According to Seneca, the best course of action is to deal with the illness as soon as you recognize it by remaining silent and controlling your emotions. Knowing your triggers will enable you to recognize when you are about to lose your temper. You can then quickly and successfully stop yourself. If you are mindful, you will be able to identify the behaviors and thoughts that make you furious. Typical causes include:

- being treated unfairly by others
- Witnessing an injustice against you or a person you care about Being rejected and other self-esteem threats
- Discrimination and prejudice

Any of the aforementioned options could serve as a trigger. Once you know what your trigger is, you can react to it quickly. You can express your rage productively if you anticipate becoming angry.

Count to five before reacting

The gap before you answer in this situation, not the number you are counting to, is the key. Seneca said that you can get rid of wrath by waiting until the initial emotion has subsided. Once it stops, the mental haze it causes dissipates, allowing you to see a little bit more clearly. The goal is to spend time in the area between the stimulus and your reaction.

I must stress that rage is a poor indicator of happiness. You become stiff and hasty as a result, which hinders your ability to think creatively. While fear may cause you to retreat, anger drives you in the direction of conflict.

It's been noted that the motivation for vengeance and payback is frequently rage. It makes sense considering that even the most intelligent people use profanity when they are upset. Remove yourself from the scenario that made you furious and wait to act until you were calm before you responded each time you felt upset. If you receive an angry email, think about it for a while before responding. If you find yourself in a fight, get out of it and, if you can, seek out another person's opinion. You're more inclined to make poor decisions when you're angry.

Art can help you relax.

Seneca believed that people with strong tempers should stay away from rigorous coursework since their minds should not be preoccupied with difficult assignments.

He advised them to engage in enjoyable activities. If you have trouble controlling your wrath, try reading poetry, listening to music, or reading novels. Let the softness and refinement of art soothe your mind. Find calming art, and it will aid your quest for mental tranquility.

This method of controlling your anger is known as "expressive theory" by psychologists. Here, you're encouraged to work out, scream, or yell to release your wrath.

Your therapist may assist you in identifying your unresolved anger issues during a treatment session. They might then advocate theatre, art, or music therapy. These are supposed to aid in your body's ability to recover from unresolved anger. You'll feel joyful and energized after seeing soothing art. Your mood will also be more stable as a result.

Imagine that you are the one who is at fault

Seneca taught his students to imagine themselves in the position of the person who is provoking their rage. We become upset because we have an incorrect perception of our value and because we are hesitant to accept the treatment we would give to others. To control your wrath, try to imagine yourself in their situation. It will bring to mind instances in which you have behaved similarly. Always ponder the following questions:

- Have I ever done something wrong? How frequently?
- Do I have a violent past?

- Have I ever mistreated someone and then regretted it?
- Have I ever deceived somebody before?

The purpose of asking this question is to encourage you to think about the situation from the viewpoint of the other party.

How do you manage your anger?

Everybody occasionally becomes irritated. The most you can achieve is to become:

- Aware of your triggers.
- Turn your attention to the perpetrators.
- Use art to help you relax.
- Wait a moment before answering.
- Think about how harmful rage is.

Healing is always preferable to exacting justice. Your time and energy will be wasted on vengeance, and you risk suffering additional harm. According to Seneca, the hurt will never survive rage.

AMOR FATI - DEALING WITH ANXIETY

'How does it help... to make troubles heavier by bemoaning them?' – Seneca.

By worrying excessively about the future, you can cause yourself anxiety. This anxiety may manifest as short-term worry over a planned event or as long-term worry about an uncertain future. The method known as "Amor Fati" that the stoics used to manage their uneasiness will be the main topic of this chapter. Amor Fati is Latin for "loving your fate." There is power in accepting whatever transpires.

People desire things to stay the same, but Nietzsche, a German philosopher who adored the idea of Amor Fati but despised stoicism, said that the secret to greatness is to endure what is required and to embrace it.

This mindset was adopted by the Stoics. A raging fire turns everything thrown into it into light and flame, as Marcus Aurelius stated in Meditations. The slave who was born with a deformed leg, Epictetus, repeated the idea, saying that happiness comes from wishing for whatever occurs to occur as it does rather than trying to make it happen the way you want. It's called "Amor Fati." It is the belief that you can take the good from any situation. No matter how difficult a moment may be, you approach it as something to enjoy rather than to avoid. You make a commitment to accept whatever occurs, but also to cherish it and allow it to improve you.

The concept of Amor Fati holds that everything will continue to happen indefinitely. Nietzsche used the phrase to describe the longing to repeat the same existence for all of eternity. It involves embracing what occurs so that, no matter what, Amor Fati is the appropriate response. If your fear of the future is keeping you from moving forward, you can, like the stoics, just "love your fate."

Keep in mind that life continues.

Think of yourself as existing in two different states: the stoic you and the nervous you. There will be layoffs at the company where you work.

You were leaving early for a doctor's appointment when you accidentally went past your boss' office. Your relationship is not going so well because your doctor told you that you might have cancer and your boyfriend believes that it is your responsibility. Because of how many challenges you face, your life will alter considerably. Because you perceive the potential change in your thoughts as either good or undesirable, the shift causes you to feel extremely apprehensive.

We feel pleasure when we experience the changes in life that are desirable. When the circumstances are bad, we feel intense agony. In any case, life continues. How much worry in your fictitious situation could you avert by telling yourself that life continues? You will always just have the now, never the past or future, no matter where you end up.

All you have is the now.

In the hypothetical scenario, I just described, we might draw the conclusion that your life is veering off course. You start to worry because of your anxiety, which keeps you up at night. You ponder whether you'll lose your job. Your partner might leave you.

What if cancer prevents you from finding employment elsewhere? You can modify some of these questions, but not all of them. Your future is ultimately out of your control. You are attempting to control the future because you are unable to deal with uncertainty, and that is the root of the problem. But what if your attention was solely on the here and now?

Accept fate

The stoic approach is to accept fate no matter what occurs. It is not the goal of Amor Fati to laze about all day and ignore reality. Making the most of each moment is important. It entails working tirelessly toward your objectives while accepting your fate when things don't turn out as you had hoped. Great if you manage to keep your job! If you lose your job, you make the best of the situation. Fantastic if you don't have cancer! If you do, you make the most of your life despite everything. Great if your partner stays! If they depart, farewell! Now that you can concentrate on yourself, you never know—you might run into someone else later.

DO YOU EMBRACE YOUR DESTINY?

Life is silently destroyed by anxiety. It is an inside bomb that can render you unconscious. However, it doesn't have to take away from your joy. Amor Fati guarantees that nothing can go wrong, and if nothing can go wrong, there is no need to fear. Anxiety does not have to drain your energy when you do not have to worry. As you can see, overcoming anxiety can be accomplished by:

- Reminding yourself that life goes on.
- Preserving the present.
- Regardless of what, accept your fate.

WHY WORRY ABOUT WHAT ISN'T REAL?
- SENECA

To be truly happy is to enjoy the present without anxiously depending on the future - not to amuse yourself with hopes and fears, but resting satisfied. The greatest blessings are within us and within our reach. He is wise who is content with his lot; who does not wish for what he does not have.' – Seneca.

Seneca stated in a letter to a friend that we suffer more from our imagination than from reality and that there are more things that are likely to frighten us than those that will demolish us. For the vast majority of worry-warts, this is true. They are less concerned with the present and more preoccupied with the possibilities of the future. Their thoughts are constantly focused on what is about to happen. They lie up at night thinking and organizing their defense against an undesired event that might occur. Because the future only exists in our imaginations, they never leave the present, despite their attempts to influence it. So what is the stoic approach to anxiety?

Get a grip on reality

Worriers overlook the fact that you can only foresee the future; you cannot live in it. It's true that some potential events can be planned for, yet our preparations do not always materialize as we had hoped. Give yourself a reality check if you find yourself in that cycle since worry has the propensity to keep you fixated on all the potential outcomes.

Remind yourself that anxiety is a liar and that you only have the present. The idea of the future is unreal. Only the here and now is real.

Recognize all of your irrational fears.

Denying the passage of time is not the goal of clinging to the notion that the future is an illusion. It involves recognizing the fleeting nature of what is occurring right now. Like a mountaintop exposed to blizzards, we are continually exposed to novelty.

No one has any influence over a blizzard, just like they have no authority over the wind. It originates from somewhere and chooses its velocity and cargo. The mountain shouldn't attempt to foresee the blizzard since it cannot. We are similar. We cannot forecast the future. All we can do is endure.

In order to overcome your unfounded anxieties about the future, always keep in mind that something is coming but you never know what or when it will strike. You will still be shooting in the dark no matter how well you plan or try to see. The only things that will exist in the future are ideas. When those thoughts seize you, confront them and then let them go. Sort out fact from conjecture. The truth, in Seneca's words, "has definite boundaries." Illusions are the product of a fearful mind; they are ambiguous and conveyed through conjecture.

Strengthen your mind

Seneca observed that some things afflict us even before they manifest and continue to do so even after they do not. This is accurate if we develop the practice of visualizing, foreseeing, or exaggerating sorrow. When there is no darkness to be discovered, the mind learns to make up fake forms of darkness. It distorts language to sow disbelief, foments resentment, and prolongs rage. Worry gets you ill, according to a study, so this behavior is not simply unpleasant. This indicates that, despite the fact that the future has not yet materialized, you worry yourself sick about it.

The remedy for this is arming your mind with the truth about reality and the cyclical nature of good fortune and bad luck. Seneca was not an easy man to live with, but he was able to handle all the bad things that happened to him. He held his position because he realized that good fortune and bad luck are unpredictable. Keep this truth in mind and be wary of the influences you let into your thinking. People are ignorant of the events' nature as well as what will happen and how they will play out. You should therefore use caution while passing judgment on fate. Sometimes a disaster you foresee materializes.

Remember that bad luck might change at any time.

The last remedy Seneca offered for anxiety dealt with luck's impermanence. There is a legend of a tiger chasing after a Buddhist guy. He plunged into an ancient well to find safety. He tightly grasped a root sticking out of the well's walls because there was a snake at the bottom. It turned out that mice were consuming the root.

When the tiger that was leaning at the well's mouth suddenly fell, landing on the snake, it appeared as though his fate had been sealed. The root's weakness caused the man to fall just in time for the snake's tail to strike him as he emerged from the well. The lesson is that adversity can strike anyone at any time, but it never lasts.

Observe carefully.

Dealing with worry does not entail numbing yourself to all the worst possibilities. Seneca opposed promoting ignorance.

He suggests that you carefully observe instead. On the other end of the scale, denying bad luck is foolish. On the other hand, you shouldn't go into panic mode at the first hint of difficulty. The trick is to walk the line between ignorance and obsession. Analyze your circumstances carefully, but leave your choices open, keeping in mind that not everything is as it seems.

HOW IS WORRY AFFECTING YOUR LIFE?

Our assessments of current or upcoming events are frequently incorrect, and our worries frequently have no justification. You can manage not to worry by:

- Keeping your feet firmly planted in reality
- Educating your mind to distinguish reality from delusion.
- Watching the future carefully.

Pondering the erratic nature of luck and bad luck.

MASTER SELF-CONTROL

'No evil propensity of the human heart is so powerful that it may not be subdued by discipline.' – Seneca.

He is calm. talked a lot about restraint. For instance, Marcus Aurelius discussed setting boundaries for comfort and consumption. Epictetus advised us to watch how we speak to avoid using filthy words. You can avoid acting on impulses and engaging in addictive behavior by exercising self-control. It aids in maintaining your attention on what matters. Focusing on what you can control, which is yourself, is the premise behind the stoics' distinction between what you can control and what you can't.

A person with self-control is less prone to become dependent on other people's or things' acceptance. They will be less subject to outside forces' control. When you exercise self-control, temptations, and triggers have less power over you, which improves your status in society. I once embarked on a 72-hour food fast after receiving support from a buddy. For three days, I was not permitted to consume anything. The first day was the worst for me, but I was able to function normally on day two. This altered my perspective on food. Before the fast, I believed that if I went without food for a day, I would pass out. I turned out to be perfectly OK. The key lesson? Many of our needs and wants are the result of thoughts in our minds rather than physical requirements or desires.

My relationship with food has never been the same after the 72-hour fast.

Knowing that I can survive for a while without eating made me feel less dependent. I've stopped stressing so much about eating. Gaining self-control helps you in that it relieves unneeded concern and tension and enables you to distinguish between actual and fictitious requirements. So how can you learn to restrain yourself like the stoics?

Give up something you enjoy for a few days.

Seneca once pondered on the celebrations taking place in Rome. The Romans delighted in all pleasures there. He argued that while refusing to engage in the festivities is brave, participating differently and without excess is much more so. His entire point was to occasionally separate oneself from luxury in order to exercise the mind. Seneca suggests setting aside a few days to live as simply as possible if you wish to develop self-control. Everything you were afraid of regarding that circumstance will become clear to you.

You may choose to refrain from using social media, the internet, or your smartphone. Try being imaginative and you'll discover your many possibilities.

Cut down on your free time.

Marcus Aurelius suggested that you might improve your self-control by setting time limits on your free time. If we want to learn from other things in the world, he emphasized, we are not designed to spend our days in leisure. Both the spiders and the bees never stop doing their jobs. Why should people differ from other animals? Not all animals are the best candidates for rigorous labor, but Marcus Aurelius had a point about living moderately, as humans should.

Before you eat, wait a bit.

This is likely the funniest and most challenging method for learning self-control out of all those suggested. Every time you serve food, take a moment to approach your plate. Don't start eating right away. When you do, chew the food a certain amount of times before swallowing.

HOW INTIMATE ARE YOU WITH DIFFICULTY?

Self-control makes us more comfortable with the things we have and familiarizes us with adversity by exposing us to situations that other people go through frequently. It helps us become less reliant on the things we think we need to be happy. The goal of these activities is to, in Seneca's words, "become intimate with poverty." In this manner, fortune won't catch you off guard. So let's sum everything up:

- Self-control prevents us from becoming dependent on other people or things.
- By undertaking any form of fast, limiting your free time, and delaying eating for a bit, you can improve your self-control.

BUILDING SELF-CONFIDENCE WITH MARCUS AURELIUS

'You want the praise of people who kick themselves every fifteen minutes, the approval of people who despise themselves. Is it a sign of self-respect to regret nearly everything you do?' – Marcus Aurelius.

The stoics held that only acts of virtue can truly make you happy. This implies that happiness cannot be obtained by material success. Most of the time, in order to create the extraordinary, we must be brave and endure almost painful things. Few things are simple to do. To get anything out of life, you have to put in the effort, be persistent, and be wise. This requires bravery. It turns out that not everyone wants to grow that courage. However, nothing is as gratifying as realizing that you are changing the world.

Regardless of your position in society, whether you are an employee or an entrepreneur, life will eventually force you to place a wager on yourself, or you will lose. That's when confidence comes into play. Even before you start to realize the benefits, it will enable you to follow your life's purpose. Self-assurance comes with practice. It is not a thought. It doesn't contain words of support. You can learn more than just intellectually. Self-assurance originates from the inside. Your actions have a bearing on it. To increase your self-assurance, the stoics advise:

Accepting who you are

Self-confidence is inextricably linked to self-acceptance. Stoics knew that if one runs from their evil side, they are simultaneously running from their light. Running from your dark side means avoiding the situations that would force you to stand alone, inspire the inner hero to take action, and encourage you to be a more moral person. The biggest sin we can make against ourselves, according to Marcus Aurelius, is to deny our shortcomings. We also disown our brilliance by doing this. Remind yourself that you are entirely and completely just the way you are if you want to feel more confident. Nobody expects you to be flawless, and you shouldn't either.

Consider accepting your weight as it is and, if necessary, working to modify it from a position of love rather than self-policing. This notion is true for all flaws. But even before you find the answer, the goal is to love yourself. Accepting the aspects of yourself that you had previously rejected does more for your self-confidence than anything.

Own your life and your decisions completely.

A poor self-perception always disempowers. It makes you abdicate account-ability for all of your decisions and behaviors. Developing self-confidence involves accepting accountability for your actions, not as the object of moral judgment but as the fundamental cause of your conduct. Teach yourself that since you have power over your life, you can pursue the things you enjoy and achieve your objectives. Even though your efforts are occasionally hindered, nobody can change your intentions. All you have to do is accommodate and adapt, as Marcus Aurelius advised.

Stand your ground on your principles.

Without standing up for what you believe in, it is impossible to live a true and courageous life. Your self-confidence increases when you stand up for what you believe. You can express your deepest emotions and convictions thanks to it. You are given the means to craft your own tale. We frequently refer to this as having a "gut feeling" since our intuition has a way of alerting us when our actions are inconsistent with our ideals. We are aware of it, but we are unable to explain it. Investigate your gut instincts and act on them when they arise. You'll get more confident as a result. As a side note, nobody will stand up for your beliefs if you don't.

What are you doing to bolster your confidence?

This chapter has demonstrated that:

- You can write your own story if you have self-confidence.
- By standing up for what you believe in, taking responsibility for your decisions and life, and accepting who you are, you can develop your self-confidence.

HOW TO CARE LESS

'I am always amazed by this: we love ourselves more than we love others, but we are more concerned about their opinion than ours. If a god came to us – or even a wise person – and prohibited us from hiding our thoughts or imagining anything without making it public, we would not last one day. That is how much we value other people's opinions rather than our own.' – Marcus Aurelius

One American sociologist stated, "I am not the person I think I am and I am not who you think I am. Our futile and irrational obsession with what others think." I am who I believe you to believe I am. You are right to think it is unusual if you do. Some people are so fixated on what other people think that they base their decisions on them. You wind up placing excessive emphasis on outside approval to the point where you are unable to experience true happiness. But what were the stoics' thoughts on this? How may stoic knowledge make you less concerned?

Explore the 'judger's' thoughts.

Imagine that someone was rating you. If all of this were true, then anytime you make a decision in life, this individual sits on a high horse and snorts at your every move. They can have different opinions on who you ought to be. That's obviously absurd, but what if it were the case? Marcus Aurelius advises trying to understand the "Judger's" perspective. Find out what kind of person they are by penetrating their soul when you receive criticism or insults from others. Then, you'll discover that you don't have to exert yourself as much to win their favor.

Marcus Aurelius was making the point that most of the time we take things that other people throw at us without questioning their justification for doing so. Would you listen to driving tips from someone you know who drives poorly? Would you consent to have someone who is heavily in debt shame you about your financial situation? You shouldn't listen to advice from someone you don't respect either. You do not have to listen to someone if you do not respect them and their decisions. Take a moment to consider those people if you wish to quit caring about what other people think. You'll discover that you're getting along just fine without straining your back to win their favor.

Contemplate Logic

Logically examining approval-seeking reveals that there is no need for concern about abandoning. Most of the time, when people detest or disapprove of us, we are not even in danger. True, it is desirable to have others adore us and it is preferable to earn likes on Facebook, but neither of these things is necessary for existence or happiness. A good reputation is a "preferred indifferent," according to the stoics. Although it is nice to be well-liked, you can still lead a good life even if you are not. Or, to put it another way, why should how people see you matter if you live well?

In his literature, Marcus Aurelius frequently showed disdain for those who sought approval by posing the question, "What's the price?" What does an audience clapping entail other than tongue-clackers? He queried. He considered public acclaim to be little more than the sound of tongues clacking. Consider this: What exactly does it mean to get likes on Facebook, for instance? Screen pixels and physical motions alone are all that can temporarily make us feel good. However, as is typical of all forms of external validation, it never actually results in our long-term contentment. It simply makes us yearn for greater approval, and what good is a life spent seeking approval?

How do you go about wanting approval?

We have less control the more we value uncontrollable factors, and we have no influence over other people's opinions. Therefore, you can simply care less by:

- Getting inside of the "judge" to recognize that they have no authority to judge you, as opposed to worrying constantly about what others think of you.
- Using reason to approach the desire for approval will help you realize that what other people think of you is none of their concern.

BE A LOSER IF NEED BE

'Think of the things you do not have as non-existent. Focus on what you have and what you value most. Think about how much you would be missing if you did not have them, but do it cautiously. Do not be so satisfied that you begin to overvalue what you have — it should not upset you to lose them.' — Marcus Aurelius

Think about what you have and what matters most to you. However, proceed with caution as you consider how much you would be missing if you did not have them. You shouldn't be so content that you start to overvalue your possessions; losing them shouldn't bother you. Marc Aurelius For the majority of individuals, this implies spending more money, whether you recently received a promotion or secured a new job with higher pay. Maybe you'll get the shoes you've been wanting. Consider signing up for a gym membership. In the end, you deserve it. Then, if you are not paying attention, one day you wake up and discover that you have 39 different ties and 50 different pairs of shoes. You own two nice cars, one of which is even nicer.

You have five distinct, equally important pairs of earbuds. You have succumbed to lifestyle creep, and the sad part is that because you no longer know what is important to you, you can never be at peace with any of it. Life is as empty as it gets. Lifestyle creep occurs when your spending increases as your income rises. For some people, it appears differently. It relates to certain people's evolving preference for finer items. It might also involve spending more on pricey hobbies, fine dining, and more rent.

You see what I mean. The issue is that lifestyle creep trumps your financial objectives. Priority is given to your new way of life over both your financial and, eventually, emotional well-being. Despite having a good income, you could end up in debt or living paycheck to paycheck. When once-luxury items start to become necessities or when you spend on pricey products and haircuts without giving it much thought, you know you're moving in this direction. The one-time costs that once hurt become more bearable. The worst aspect is that you start to believe you are improving while actually hurting yourself. You may keep yourself in check so that you are no longer ruled by things by using Epictetus' life advice:

Being a loser

The image of a "loser" is a shadow created by stories of victors or individuals with fame, power, and wealth in today's world. However, the success of the Stoics went beyond wealth, power, and notoriety. Being a loser was nothing to be embarrassed by, in Epictetus' opinion. If you call someone a loser today, you are rejecting them. It is a racial, sexist, gendered, or other type of divide–based insult. The loser ultimately loses status. However, the word did not carry the same level of disdain for the stoics. The stoics didn't care about wealth, fame, or power. You too can be. Consider everything you own as an extra that would be lovely to have but that you could go without. Never give up your ability to make decisions in exchange for money or status. The stoic does not view life as a competition. Keep your words, behaviors, and ideas in harmony with nature to win the contest. As long as you maintain your integrity, anything else that happens to you will be a triumph. If you succeed in the test of virtue, even if you lose your home, friends, health, or position, you can still consider yourself victorious and even view such losses as advantages.

Consider the passing of your heroes.

A stoic will understand that not everyone who is labeled as a "loser" actually is one. Since virtue is the only good, the one who does not uphold virtue is the loser, not the person who lacks things, position, or money. The Stoics, however, did not stop there.

They suggested regular reflection on the deaths of your heroes because they knew that human weakness may deceive you into inverting your priorities. By doing this, you protect yourself from the propensity of human nature (as well as other outside causes) to derail your pursuit of virtue. Socrates, Plato, Diogenes, Heracles, Patroclus, Odysseus, and other figures were heroes of the Stoics. They idolized those who exemplified morality. Your modern-day heroes can be persons who lead the life you aspire to lead or who have accomplished things that inspire you.

Epictetus advised you to contemplate death on a regular basis. You maintain perspective balance by doing this. Your hold on your possessions becomes less as you become aware that even the best among us are only men at best. If your hero has passed away, then you might remind yourself that they passed away not long after their accomplishments. If they were still living, you would be aware of their impending demise. This can help you determine what you should actually care about if you keep it in mind every day. Do you let your life's circumstances define you? By caring less, you offer yourself the freedom to not be victimized by events. You begin to prepare a place of honor within yourself so that, in the event of adversity, you can seek refuge there. Your method is to turn into a loser. thinking about the passing of your heroes.

98

THEIR OPINIONS ARE UNIMPORTANT

"The person who lives as he wishes, who cannot be compelled, obstructed, or coerced, and whose impulses cannot be thwarted, is truly free."

He always gets what he wants and never has to put up with anything he would rather not deal with. How often did you worry about what other people thought of you before a meeting? How many times has your dread of what other people think incapacitated you? Have you ever given yourself permission to change how you act in reaction to what you thought other people would think or say? People's perceptions used to have a big impact. When we were hunters and gatherers in the past, staying safe required relying on the judgments of others.

We needed other people like us because it was always possible to be killed or banished from the tribe. You would be better off if you finished your task and followed everyone else's lead. Anybody who broke the rules was an outcast and would perish by themselves. However, circumstances have changed, and your ability to survive does not depend on what others think. So why do you still let other people's opinions affect how you feel about yourself? The stoics' position on this is as follows:

Review the conceptual model of your life.

Contrary to then, when we lived off of fruits and meat and knew everyone we met, the internet today connects us on a global scale.

Over 40% of individuals on the earth have access to the internet. Thanks to technology like email and social media, we continue to be connected on a level that is beyond the capacity of our reptile brains. That brain still wants to be accepted, even though the tribe won't reject it. Even when it is done on purpose, worrying about other people's opinions prevents us from doing our best work. It begins to produce issues. Essentially, your perception of existence is erroneous or outdated.

According to Epictetus, true freedom entailed the ability to do as you choose, when you desire, without hindrance from others — provided that you do it, of course, within the bounds of what is appropriate. It's hard to win everyone over. There will always be different opinions about how the world should function. These opinions may occasionally be at odds with your own. This does not mean that you should keep your ideas to yourself. Focus on what you're doing. Does it really matter what other people think? If everyone is taken into consideration, what they say matters. However, you must never let the actions or words of others dictate your own behavior.

So maybe you hear from people who disagree with your opinions. Or maybe they're gossiping about you behind your back. Is it really so crucial? Epictetus believes that the answer is "no." It's easy to recall Epictetus' catchphrase, "If they really knew my flaws and who I am, they would have said worse." The key is to prioritize your own development over what others may think. You could respond to those people. You could try to persuade them otherwise, but in the end, your behavior will speak for itself. Conflict will always exist. Everyone goes through it.

According to Seneca, if you never face challenges in life, you will never reach your full potential. The best thing to focus on is your actions, not the opposition. Marcus Aurelius asserted that inner tranquility develops when one quits giving concern about what other people think, say, or do. Focus on your work and let it do the talking. H? The truly free person, according to Epictetus, never has to deal with matters they would rather avoid. So there you have it:

Update your mental picture of life and pay attention to your behaviors

if you want to escape being bound by other people's perceptions. I'll give you many more reasons in the next chapter why you shouldn't think too much about what other people think. How have you been subjecting yourself to other people's perspectives so far?

REASONS NOT TO WORRY WHAT OTHERS THINK

'He gains much time, he who does not consider what his neighbor says, thinks, or does, but only what he himself does, to make it holy and just.' – Marcus Aurelius

The stoics believed that worrying about what other people think is a waste of time. Most individuals care about other people's opinions, but if you do it to the point where you ignore your own or make decisions that are harmful to you, it can be difficult for your well-being. You need to discover internal validation if you want to feel happy and confident. Here are five stoics' arguments for why you shouldn't care what people think:

The opinions of others have no bearing on your inherent worth.

What they think is merely a thought in their mind, as Seneca famously put it.

Just that. The opinions of other people do not alter who you are. However, if I'm being completely honest, we naturally crave the approval of others, therefore it might be challenging to put this simple concept into practice. Our upbringing prepares us for this since our parents applaud the child who follows their interests. Teachers applaud students' compliance at school.

When we start working later, our coworkers do what they always did and stick to the script. Few individuals ever stop to think that our essential worth is unaffected by anyone else's opinion.

Do other people's thoughts make you a worse or better person? You don't, though. Your value and worth are unaffected by what other people may think. Therefore, you can save yourself from stress if you quit thinking about what other people will think. You begin to concentrate on developing personally. You give up attempting to find anything wrong with people as a coping method.

You give attention to who you wish to be.

Your imagination is endless.

In the end, only you get to decide who you are. Only you have the power to decide who you will become. It doesn't affect who you are if someone doesn't agree with your decisions or doesn't like you. When this reality sinks in, you understand that no one can limit your creativity or imagination. When you connect with the things that motivate and inspire you, everything only becomes better.

You gauge success by your own standards.

I must emphasize that having less concern does not mean ignoring other people's viewpoints entirely. It is that, even if you do listen to others, you do so voluntarily rather than under duress, and you only take into account what they have to say if it is accurate. So, how do you go about doing this? How do you resist letting other people's views influence you? How do you move on after someone calls you names? How can praise keep you from becoming conceited?

Spend some time outlining your objectives so that you may better understand what you want from life. What other people think of your route won't matter once you are sure of it. The more you let go of other people's opinions, the more your route becomes obvious, and the more you let go of other people's ideas, the clearer your road becomes. Everything is related.

Others are burdened by baggage

When you are preoccupied with someone else's opinion, you put them in a superior position to yourself. You disregard their human nature. The reality is that other people tend to transfer their problems onto us. In some cases, people do it without even realizing it. Worrying about their opinions is pointless since they can be condemning you because of a decision they made that they later regretted. The key here is to let go of what you cannot verify and to be curious about the verifiable facts.

Think of yourself as a presenter at work. During the meeting, nobody says anything, but later you overhear a colleague's comment that they didn't enjoy your presentation. Are you trying to offend me? Does their viewpoint affect how you present? No. Imagine approaching them and finding out what they thought was lacking in your presentation. They claim that they would have changed the PowerPoint background. Or perhaps one of the pictures you used was particularly upsetting. You cannot change these things because they are merely opinions.

Imagine, though, that they informed you that your presentation lacked sufficient research. Perhaps they observed an inaccurate graph. You can check these things off your list and update them. The following time, you can correct your graph and conduct more study. In this situation, you should express gratitude for your colleague's candor. Learning to distinguish between fact and opinion is a skill that the Stoics promoted. Next time you watch the news, choose a newspaper and divide it into two columns: one for facts and one for opinions. As the speaker speaks, pay attention and note what you hear in each of the columns. Take note of how many times they present opinions as facts. You will gain mastery of the stoic ability to distinguish between opinion and fact with this exercise.

You are in charge of your emotions.

You are not truly in control of your emotions when you are preoccupied with other people's perceptions. They do. They now have influence over the world inside of you. You must assume responsibility if you ever catch yourself blaming others for how you feel about yourself. Your reaction to other people's words is entirely up to you. Instead, opt to improve and learn.

What do you use to determine your sense of worth?

According to Buddhist philosophy, attachment is the cause of all suffering. If you put your self-worth on what other people think of you, you are setting yourself up for serious unhappiness. You're turning yourself into a victim. The reasons from this chapter for letting go of other people's perspectives are summarized as follows:

- What they believe has no bearing on who you are.
- Some people are toting bags.
- You decide what success means to you.
- You are incredibly creative.
- You regain emotional control.

RECOVERING FROM A BREAKUP

'Never say of anything 'I have lost it but, 'I have returned it.' – Epictetus

Even the best of us experience it. Today, as a couple, we are blissful, madly in love, and walking hand in hand to our favorite place the next day, there is a fight. There is an error.

Someone is running late. Soon after a harsh remark is made, we must learn to live without the person we have come to love. Then what? When the fabric of your relationship is shredded, what do you do? Once more, the stoics had advice for those who were recovering after a breakup.

I should point out that over the years, the idea of romance and love has evolved. Ancient Greek dating customs were very dissimilar from modern dating practices. However, some human emotions, such as rage, aversion, hunger, love, and lust, have remained constant. Nature, unlike us, has time. So, despite the rapid advancement of society, our physiology has not substantially changed. For this reason, stoicism can still be useful in coping with heartbreak.

It's true that we now have more knowledge about how the brain functions, but this does not make ancient knowledge worthless.

But before getting into it, let's break down what happens following a breakup and why it hurts so much. It's quite intense to fall in love. Your body makes substances that are euphoric. Soon enough, all your thoughts are focused on the person you love.

You can bond thanks to these compounds. There are other names for them, including the "honeymoon phase." After that stage passes, you start to see the other person more realistically, yet you still have a strong bond with them. It is what a breakup obstructs. Do you have to endure suffering eternally, then? (It frequently feels that way. The response is "no." The rational mind, according to the stoics, can ease heartache.

Modify your worldview

Even while you cannot wish the grief away, altering some ideas will help you cope with the reality of the split. You'll feel at ease with your new situation as a result. According to the Stoics, you can modify the following beliefs:

I want them to be content.

Clinginess can occasionally be a result of this belief. People in today's world will merely inform you that "there are many fish in the sea." It is true, yet after a split, it is difficult to accept. You struggle to understand why anyone would want to replace your beloved with you. Furthermore, the issue is not resolved by that adage. Regardless of how many fish there are, fish are still an outside reality.

Theoretically, even though there are lots of fish, you might never catch any of them. It is something you are powerless over.

The mistake you are making is believing that your happiness depends on the outside if you suffer after a breakup because you feel like you need your ex to be happy. Stoicism strongly disagrees with this. The stoics held that virtue is all that is necessary for happiness in life. If so, getting into a relationship, getting married, and falling in love is not necessary for your happiness. These variables are untrustworthy. You will be happy if you focus on leading a moral life.

I have a right to them.

Most of the time, you are not aware that you have adopted this viewpoint, but eventually, you begin to view the person you love as an entitlement. You fail to recognize the treasure that their time and affection are. This notion frequently goes hand in hand with envy and loss anxiety. So you feel betrayed when they break up with you. You believe that the cause for the separation was unfair. You might feel aggrieved if there is a divorce because your ex-spouse decided against being with you until death do you part. If there was any cheating, you feel betrayed.

The odd thing is that monogamy and sexual exclusivity have not always been the norm. They are ideas that societal structures are forced to accept, and they are frequently passed down together with religious beliefs.

If left unchecked, they eventually feed your sense of entitlement and dread of loss. Epictetus, a stoic philosopher, has some thoughts on how to approach this concept after a breakup. He claimed that you just returned love rather than losing it. Anyone who gives has the authority to take away. You are less likely to feel offended by the fact that your ex-spouse stopped things if you think of them in that way.

I'll never move past them.

It may seem impossible to move past your ex after a breakup because of the agony involved, but time truly does heal all wounds. According to Marcus Aurelius, certain things rush us into life while others rush us out of it. A portion of the present has already passed. The world is continually being rebuilt by change, just as eternity is being created by the relentless march of time. You can cope with the anguish you experience. You need not struggle against it. Just recognize it and give it some time. Keep in mind that dealing with sadness involves both being active in the world and taking a quiet moment to be with it. Accept what you are feeling, put up with the separation it will cause, and let time do its work.

Seneca once wrote to his mother to let her know that he was missed. He comforted her, telling her to give her sorrow time. Nothing is more harmful than taking drugs too soon, he declared. You will be able to handle the cures that would enable grief to be touched if you wait until it exhausts itself by its own violence and weakens due to time. Seneca was telling his mother to let herself cry, to put it another way. Allow yourself to cry when thinking about your heartbreak. Stay human. After the shock has subsided, cover the wound with a bandage.

Avoid making matters worse.

There is a law concerning holes:

Stop digging if you find yourself in one.

Even though it seems straightforward, most individuals break it after a heartbreak. What do you do if you feel wronged? For the majority of individuals, anger comes first, after which they flail and make matters worse. Seneca believed that when we complain, it only makes the situation worse. Avoid letting your anger enter the equation and make things worse. Avoid acting simply because you can. Give up digging. Do not sign up for as many dating apps as possible. Do not rush into a relationship. Avoid using social media. Always keep in mind that you have a choice. You might concentrate on how you were harmed, or you can learn from the relationship and appreciate its positive aspects.

Don't look for someone to blame.

Epictetus strongly discouraged looking for people or things to blame.

He counsels you to stop looking for a scapegoat and accomplish what you need to do rather than wailing to God to explain why your heart had to break. Our life can be divided into two categories, according to the author Robert Greene: Dead time and lively time.

While you are inactive and waiting during dead time, you are learning, acting, and making the most of your time during alive time. Every minute that is not under your control passes into either alive time or dead time. Every part of you wants to whine about your situation after a breakup, but this is the attitude that will waste time. Keep in mind that you cannot get that time back. Choose a lively time in its place. Change your tone to "This is an opportunity for me to learn and grow."

Seek assistance

When coping with a breakup, it's typical for people to feel guilty about requiring assistance. Marcus Aurelius encourages us not to be ashamed about asking for assistance. Like every soldier in combat, you have a responsibility. You need the assistance of your fellow soldiers if you are hurt. Nobody anticipates you owning all the resources required to address every issue you encounter. Observe that. Then go ahead and request assistance. You don't have to handle everything by yourself. Simply ask for assistance.

Concentrate on the now

Your life reflection can crush you after a breakup. Pay attention to Marcus Aurelius and refrain from visualizing every negative scenario that could possibly occur. Consider your present and consider how you can make it through. Just consider it:

What were the scariest, most dangerous situations you have ever encountered? How did you get past them? By seeing past the slim chances, you will discover that you prevail. Even in this situation, when your heart is breaking, try not to think negatively. In the midst of sadness, it may be easier to zoom in and focus on the small elements of life than the larger picture. Negative thoughts are driven out of your head when you concentrate on the here and now. It's similar to how a man walking a tightrope doesn't consider how high up or how far away the end is. He merely advances one step at a time.

ALWAYS LOVE

This is possibly the most radical stoic advice for coping with love-related heartbreak. As Seneca put it, "If you want to be loved, love." It is simple to hate after experiencing heartbreak because hate shifts responsibility. It absolves you of accountability. When you are preoccupied with seeking retribution or investigating the wrongs of others, it diverts your attention, preventing you from doing much else. But does this bring you any closer to mental tranquility? No. You are merely kept in a loop by it.

Love is the better reaction. Love the person who disappointed you. Love the people who turned you down. Love the person who impulsively stole your heart. Love everyone because ultimately, the love you give is the love you receive. Be motivated by people who, like Martin Luther King Jr., advocated for the freedom of love over the burden of hatred. Hatred is a cancer that destroys your life from the inside out. It is a potent acid that eats away at your best qualities. Hatred never helps a situation in life turn out better. But love improves practically everything. Who knows, maybe some of the love you offer will come back to you.

ARE YOU STUCK IN A LOOP, OBLIVIOUS TO THEIR PAIN?

Because of the manner that heartbreak may make us blind, I have taken the time to talk about it. After a breakup, everything you know to be significant is hidden from view. But we are elastic and infinitely adaptable. By:

- Modifying our beliefs, we can apply stoic wisdom to learn and advance from breakups.
- Not escalating the situation.
- Assuming accountability.
- Seeking assistance.
- Keeping the present in mind and deciding to always choose love over hate.

HOW TO NOT GET OFFENDED

'Anyone who can anger you masters you; he can anger you because you allow yourself to be disturbed by him.' – Epictetus

According to the Stoics, choosing not to be offended by what other people do will prevent you from being so. Your interpretation will determine the offense. Instead of taking offense, you might be kind to others and show your independence. An instance of this in action is a tale about Mahatma Gandhi that was circulated in South Africa.

Gandhi was out on a stroll with his buddy Charles Freer Andrews in a Johannesburg neighborhood. People started shouting racist chants at them and harassing them. Andrews had his doubts, but Gandhi persisted, preferring to turn the other cheek. Gandhi retorted, "You will find that there is room for us all," in response to one of the men shouting, "We are cleaning up our neighborhood."

Gandhi experienced racial discrimination; nevertheless, you probably have many other opportunities to be offended.

We now have incredibly easy access to information thanks to the information era.

Online college courses are available. You can study computing, philosophy, and art. You can use a YouTube guide to fix your boiler. The world of today offers a wealth of opportunities for learning. But there is a drawback to all this connectivity. The opinions of other people affect us more than they did in the past.

It turns out that disagreement, dispute, and debate are effective at grabbing our attention. The debate is what we like most. We like choosing teams.

This is, in a way, primitive. So much so that some people choose their side so strongly that they become blind to the real world. Thanks to Facebook, Instagram, and YouTube, news organizations are now facing competition from websites they never would have considered to be a threat in the past. The public is not interested in traditional news sources.

With all of them, offense immediately comes to mind. You come across an offensive photo while browsing Instagram. You get offended when a YouTube video criticizes something you adore. Friction is caused by differences of opinion. The outcome is a culture of anger. However, how do you get away from it? The stoics have a strategy for achieving happiness:

Make opinions less personal.

When you identify too closely with someone else's viewpoint, you become insulted. It occurs when you interpret someone else's viewpoint as an attack because you took it personally. However, unless the opinion is about you, it is usually just that—an opinion. Reminding yourself that something is not personal when someone expresses their viewpoint can help you avoid taking offense. They are merely outlining their values. A difference in values is not a form of aggression. Values are created based on knowledge and experience. Thus, such a distinction is, at most, a sign of a different life.

You may have a respectful conversation about topics like sports, religion, nuclear power, and other topics without offending anyone when you learn to depersonalize beliefs. You are able to do this because you are aware that when someone has a different viewpoint from your own, it is only their way of expressing their ideas. Furthermore, a person's viewpoint is not always indicative of reality or the truth. Frequently, it's just their viewpoint based on their personal experiences.

Recognize the distinctions

The impulse to alter other people's viewpoints is a defining feature of the outrage culture. It sounds as if you can't have a disagreement and coexist in the same environment. Have you ever watched footage of individuals reacting negatively to social movements? Although many modern activists have noble intentions, the way they carry out their campaigns renders them ineffective. Screaming and shouting are ineffective methods for influencing people's opinions. Accepting that there can be disagreements is a necessary component of not taking offense. If you want to influence others' opinions, use your argument rather than your voice because you have no authority to do it. Outrage just leads to further outrage and pain. The next time someone expresses an opinion you disagree with, try to see it for what it is and try to understand where they are coming from rather than getting upset and defensive.

Control yourself.

In the end, controlling oneself is the key to not being offended. Marcus Aurelius counseled showing compassion to those who have offended you. He claimed that when someone hurts you, consider the benefit you could derive from it; this will make you feel more sympathetic. You'll realize that your perception of right and wrong may not be the same as theirs, in which case you should feel sympathy for them. You lose power when you decide to take offense. You begin to nurture ill will. On the other side, kindness is unstoppable. Just make sure it's genuine.

What can a cruel person do if all of your responses are polite, gently correcting him? continues Marcus Aurelius. What happens if you guide him without accusing him? Epictetus recommended self-control and morality as a defense against being offended. It might be the case that you were treated improperly by someone, but it is something only they can judge. Your responsibility is to treat him rightfully. You should be worried about this.

Do you easily offend?

Being non-offended is a practice in self-mastery because being offended is a decision you make. Choose not to be offended the next time you have something to be offended about. Attempt to identify the offense. Remember that you can only alter yourself, and forgive them for their transgressions. You have done well if you can forgive an infraction. Decide not to allow other people to manipulate you. Let's review what the stoics had to say about being offended now:

- The opinions of other people are an expression of their ideals and should not be interpreted personally.

- Individual differences are OK.
- Attacking is a decision. Instead, choose kindness.

THREE STOIC WAYS OF LETTING GO

'A philosopher expects all hurt and benefit from himself. A proficient one censures no one, accuses no one, praises no one, and blames no one.' – Epictetus

A skilled one does not criticize, condemn, exalt, or point the finger at anyone.

– Epictetus In prior chapters, we argued that letting go is a prerequisite for finding serenity. We've covered how to let go of things you can't change in great detail. But precisely how do you let go? Many individuals want to lead happy lives, but many are unsure of how to do so. To help you live happily, stoic wisdom offers three exercises and wisdom that are motivated by how the world functions. They consist of:

Modify your conclusions.

The stoics held that nothing that occurs to you or around you is by definition good or harmful. Events are morally neutral. Your mind decides if something is nice or harmful. Why is this important? because we have little influence over the majority of the events in our lives. We only have control over our judgment. According to Epictetus, how experiences affect us depends on how we evaluate them. You will lead a happier life if you adopt a mind state that is compatible with nature. Be careful not to judge things that are out of your control.

Live morally

Stoic ethics has always included both virtues and vices. They relate to the stoic philosophy of living in harmony with nature. It is a vice if it goes against nature. It is a virtue if it is in harmony with nature. Happiness will always follow virtue. Follow the principles of wisdom, moderation, courage, and fairness if you want to learn how to let go. When there is a lot of room for a moral grey area, make decisions based on intelligence and the pursuit of virtue.

Reduced expectations

High expectations deceive us into hoping for a positive outcome from circumstances beyond our control. You will undoubtedly be let down if you approach life and the outside world in this way. For instance, you will be dissatisfied if you expect your father to be supportive, affectionate, and respectful of your choices but he turns out to be flaky, aloof, and dismissive. Are you disappointed because of your father or are you disappointed because of your expectations? Epictetus asserts that you do not have a right to the good. You only have a right to what is naturally yours; you are not entitled to anything else. You suffer if you want more from nature than it can provide. This anguish will come from within. Similar ideas were held by Marcus Aurelius. He had to cope with difficult people in his lifetime, and he was all too aware that having an overly upbeat view would lead to disappointment. He prepared himself for each day by anticipating others' disloyalty, malice, ungratefulness, and selfishness.

This is a useful practice to do in order to adjust your expectations and be less bothered by what happens to you.

What are you clinging to that is not yours to bear?

What are the things you hold on to that hurt you emotionally? How are you causing yourself more suffering? According to the Stoics, you can learn to let go by

- controlling your expectations,
- leading a moral life,
- altering your opinions of the world and the events that happen in it.

STOIC WISDOM FOR MENTAL TOUGHNESS

'You have power over your mind – not outside events. Realize this, and you will find strength.' – Marcus Aurelius

Have you ever felt that you fell short of expectations? Have you ever thought that you don't think you can succeed in life?

Do you constantly stress and worry yourself to death, presumably feeling too much is being put on your shoulders? Do you ever question the choices you make? You probably fall prey to a weak mental determination if you said "yes" to any of these questions. The greatest course of action for you right now is to step outside of your comfort zone and strengthen your mind.

A person with strong mental fortitude can combat and control worries, doubts, and other situations that get in the way of their success.

They protect you from any setbacks like a fortress. We've all felt terror at times. Even while living in fear is a natural aspect of being human, only the psychologically fragile do so. Having mental toughness can enable you to overcome obstacles and confront your concerns. It makes sense why athletes are frequently urged to maintain their composure and consistency despite the pressure. The main motivation is for them to have a strong mind. But is mental toughness just a tool for athletes?

The ability to persevere when others start to give up is what separates truly great individuals from the general populace. It is their capacity to stick to their principles even under the most trying circumstances. It is their perseverance in the face of difficulty, and this perseverance calls for mental toughness. As they negotiate their course forward, they must embrace uncertainty and discomfort. Anyone can achieve greatness if they make the effort to learn this skill.

Remember that brilliance is not always equated with what society generally recognizes as success. According to Seneca, success happens to the untalented and the lowly, but what makes a great person truly exceptional is their capacity to overcome the crises and misfortunes of daily life. The key idea here is that it's possible to be born with advantages and appear successful in other people's eyes without actually accomplishing much on your own.

You must develop the perseverance to stick it out if you want to be more than a shell and develop the qualities that distinguish the genuinely successful. You must possess the capacity to accept extended periods of challenging learning and tolerate rejection. Simply put, there are no shortcuts. The ability to successfully navigate challenges is ultimately the only method to acquire mental toughness. Being mentally tough takes work. The best part is that the odds start to change in your favor as you start to grow it. You merely need to identify what is viable and worthwhile to pursue to completion. It turns out that the stoics were also aware of the immeasurable worth of this skill. They provide guidance on enhancing resilience, such as:

Get creative

Epictetus disapproved of lecturing his pupils about proper conduct.

If someone doesn't fully comprehend your life's circumstances, what counsel can they really provide you? – however, nobody ever does. Developing an adaptive mind, in his opinion, is preferable. A mind that can accept any situation will lead you off-course. It won't be in a desperate search for guidance. It will choose its own course. The educational system in place now is hierarchical. Every class has procedures, and every course has a curriculum. If you can learn to be organized, you are regarded as the best. However, as soon as you leave the classroom, you realize that life is not that regimented.

For instance, conditions alter frequently during work. You begin working on a project in the morning, but by midday, a news item has changed the situation so drastically that you must change your plans. The inability of your mind to handle ambiguity is a serious drawback. You will struggle not only at work but also in life if you require detailed instructions and can't function without being given defined tasks. Life doesn't have scripts, after all. Life is more about being creative than it is about following a checklist of instructions. There is no perfect blueprint.

There would still be so many variables and subtleties in your life, even if you modeled it after the life of someone you respect, so you would need to be inventive. You can't get away from it. You must develop the ability to adjust and maintain momentum despite obstacles. You have the chance to learn how to solve problems every day, no matter what your circumstance. Utilizing your life experience as a resource is how you demonstrate mental toughness.

Spend some alone time

Seneca believed that a man's capacity to put his goals on hold and spend time with himself is the surest indication of a rational mind. Nothing is more accurate. The majority of the time, disorganized and chaotic thinking passes for busyness. Learn to like being by yourself if you want to develop your mental fortitude. Accept reflection. You can only learn what is really important to you and what you want to do with your life this way. You will be more focused if you complete this as soon as possible.

You can connect with yourself and work "in the zone" by reflecting. A calm and concentrated mind produces the much-desired "flow." People who constantly switch between diversions are unable to develop the resilience they need to stand out. Establish a sanctuary in your head where you may go to block out the world and focus on your task. Make alone time a priority to improve your stability and resilience.

Less consumption, greater creation

Sustained immersion in any field of study is taxing and exhausting for many people. Few people are able to tolerate performing the same thing repeatedly. Some people are so afraid of the demands that they never even consider starting. In the end, they decide to prioritize illusions and diversions over their dreams. On the other hand, they never experience the rewards saved for those who decide to choose to perfect themselves and their craft. Without a willingness to finish whatever you start, there is no such thing as mental strength. It will beckon you to keep turning up every day, whether it's running your own business or producing your own work.

Giving up is simpler to do. There are many reasons to tap out, yet doing so is a betrayal of who you are. You abdicate responsibility for meaning production to others. Because, according to the stoics, what you produce and what you release into the world will be what defines you.

WHAT DEFINES YOU?

What areas of your vision are you compromising for deceptions and distractions? What commitments have you made? how you develop mental toughness, according to the Stoics are as followings.

- Spending time alone
- Increases one's inventiveness.
- Putting forth more than you take in.

WHEN LIFE HURTS, STOP CLINGING TO IT

'It is not insults or ill language that is insulting, but the principle interpreting them. When anyone provokes you, be assured that it is your own opinion that provokes you.' – Epictetus

Epictetus noted that we become burdened by our overabundance of concerns in life. He counseled people to cease caring about things that don't matter and instead focus their attention on the important things. However, how can you judge what is important and what is not?

It turns out that what really matters is determined by how we see ourselves in a constantly changing context. There are things you can alter and things you cannot change, despite what you may believe. Care for what you can change instead of worrying about what you can't alter offers you strength. If you hold on to those disempowering things, it gets worse.

Knowing when to let go and when to hang on is a crucial component of mental toughness, but it can be challenging to do. Epictetus, for instance, mentioned going into exile. Nothing could have stopped him from being exiled with a grin, but he would have been in misery if he had held to the notion that exile was a tragedy. He was adept at knowing where his decisions ended and others' began. He made the decision to disregard what was not up to him. His philosophy may be summed up in two words: let go of what you cannot control and do not cling to what hurts. He offered strategies for doing this, such as:

Don't hold on to items you've borrowed.

It seems normal to develop attachments to both the people and the things we spend a lot of time with. We keep adding a possessive component to love and attachment. Then, for instance, when someone leaves our presence, we feel betrayed and abandoned. Even worse, because we live in continual anxiety that they may leave, we lose the person numerous times in our imaginations before we actually lose them. In that way, our imagination is deceiving. When you cling to something or someone, the possibility of their departure exposes you to the ongoing pain of dealing with it. In certain circumstances, your existence revolves around preventing the separation because you are so frightened of losing them. The same cycle applies to power.

Speaking of power, the Greek philosopher Epicurus claimed that it is an insatiable appetite. It makes sense that once you have power, you want more. Power corrupts us, and because we want more of it or don't want to give it up, it makes us miserable and suffers. Ironically, even while having authority gives you the impression that you are in charge, you are not. Power can be acquired or transferred at any time. Because of this, anyone who fights for it is a fool. You have to become used to impermanence if you want to live the stoic way, in harmony with nature.

Consider people, authority, and things as a dinner party, as Epictetus did. When anything is placed before you at a dinner party, you choose a small amount and pass the remainder. You cannot halt the progression of events. You never even consider it. You wait for a glass of wine to come your way, and eventually, it does. Apply this to people, authority, and things. Going with the flow is living in harmony with nature. Accept visitors with love if they come to you.

If they go, let them go while continuing to love them. Accept power and possessions if you receive them. If they are removed, that is life.

This mindset will make you more resilient to the hurt of loss. It will alter how you view the things you adore. Consider everything as borrowed rather than believing you are entitled to it or that you own it. If a loved one passes away, be grateful for the time you had with them and acknowledge that they are now with God. This mentality will also encourage you to look after your possessions while you still have them. You are simply a guest in a motel after all. Holding on to what is borrowed can only make things worse for you. Live your life such that you can always let go of what you have.

Avoid adhering to the viewpoints of others

Many people will go to great lengths to win others' favor. In today's technologically connected world, it is worse. It's true that when people think positively of us, we benefit. For instance, if we are likable, we can easily make friends. It might be simpler to locate a romantic partner and other things if we are attractive. The stoics, however, believed that external causes should always submit to our composure. For instance, we shouldn't be upset if we don't receive an invitation to a party, especially if we don't get along with the host. Although being invited provides advantages, such as attendance and appreciation, if we don't want to spend time and effort getting to know someone, we shouldn't be upset if we aren't invited. There is no way around it.

No matter how content you may feel in the moment, striving to be liked drains your energy. For the sake of your inner serenity, you don't laud those you'd prefer to avoid. In reality, calm and that very thing are incompatible. According to Epictetus, if suffering scorn and mockery is the price you pay for serenity, liberation, and composure, then so be it. If we are at peace, we must be content with being viewed as dumb since, at the end of the day, we have no control over other people's perceptions. We only have control over how they impact us. What good does it do you to cling to other people's opinions when you allow yourself to be led by them?

Don't cling to concepts and results

Every time you attempt to manipulate the universe, you fail. You will also fail in your attempt to alter the status quo. But the majority of the time, we are preoccupied with what ought to be occurring right now, what ought to have happened in the past, and what ought to happen in the future. But the more we fight against what is, the more painful life will be.

In support of this notion, Epictetus describes how we ought to treat a servant. While a servant should be obedient, he or she should act in a manner that prevents constant obedience. People are people, thus it is expected that they won't always behave as expected. Epictetus was attempting to make the point that we shall be at peace if we understand that the servant won't always behave as we like. Anything can benefit from this thought.

You can't always count on the world to be kind, for instance. You may find certain people to be offensive. The truth that someone will always offend someone else will not change if you silence them. That is just how people are. Therefore, toying with the notion of an unoffensive environment would only lead to disillusionment, while imposing it will have the opposite effect.

Being kind to yourself first, which is something you can manage, is a better strategy. Others might imitate your behavior, but that is entirely up to them. We are not in a position to control how the world comes and goes. We lose if we cling to them. We succeed if we accept them and live well despite them.

Epictetus taught people how to let go. He advised not clinging to: You will be happier and stronger if you do not.

- Ideas and results.
- the views of other people.
- items that have been lent.

BUILD MENTAL FORTITUDE

'When you arise in the morning, think what a precious privilege it is to be alive – to breathe, to think, to enjoy, to love.' – Marcus Aurelius

Sometimes, people confuse solitude with tenacity. But there is a significant distinction between the two. When you isolate, you physically distance yourself from other people and the outside world in search of a stronghold to protect yourself in. Serial self-isolators eventually come to feel helpless and impotent, thinking that everything going on outside their castle is too much for them to manage. They feel weak and incapable of handling things.

Unfortunately, people miss out on a lot of life events because they are frightened to deal with evil.

Strength is an alternative to self-isolation. You could decide to strengthen your mental faculties so that you are better equipped to deal with unpleasant individuals and situations. In this manner, nothing negative would prevent you from leading a happy life. This method of life in the world was promoted by the Stoics. For them, developing fortitude meant developing the mental fortitude necessary to lead moral lives. Stoic ideas can help you develop a mind that is less likely to run away when adversity arises and more inclined to live life to the fullest. Here are a few of those guidelines:

Examine your outlook on life.

Everybody has some core beliefs that guide our daily actions. Some of them are to blame for the upsetting life circumstances that make our lives appear intolerably difficult. According to Seneca, it is not life itself that hurts us; rather, it is our beliefs. The reasoning for it is that we frequently associate our happiness with particular expectations, and when those expectations aren't met, we feel unhappy.

Seneca delved deeper into this concept in a letter to his pal Serenus. Serenus desired an end to disrespectful behavior among people. He heard Seneca explain why his viewpoint was incorrect. Serenus wished that all people were kind, but this is not feasible.

We frequently need to alter the way we perceive the world, just like Serenus. By implementing this change, we prevent the unneeded suffering of opposition.

People that are violent, self-centered, and nasty abound throughout life. When we come to terms with this reality, we can go through life peacefully. Seneca continued by saying that if we do not know how to die well, we cannot live well.

He believed that acceptance of death's inevitability is a prerequisite for mental fortitude. Nothing will surprise you if you are aware that death is a real possibility.

Limit your dislikes and desires

According to Epictetus, maintaining control over our aversions and cravings is the foundation of mental fortitude. Most people start their days or engage in situations expecting particular results. Although it's not always a terrible thing, this has repercussions. According to Epictetus, a person is truly happy and at peace when he suppresses desire and focuses his aversion exclusively on things he can control. This holds true in all facets of life. Consider this: Being a slave to something you cannot control. Your mood is usually erratic when it depends on others.

Epictetus counseled us to take an impartial stance toward anything outside of our control. Building a healthy scorn for what you cannot control is a necessary component of mental toughness. In actuality, this appears as not wanting the praise and acceptance of others, not being afraid of losing things, and concentrating exclusively on your activities.

Just be good.

One of the finest stoics is Chrysippus. Sadly, none of the 700 or so books he authored have survived. But his ideas persisted. He developed the stoic ethical framework by proposing the notion that everything we do is intended to make our lives happier. To get there, we must know what is good from what is evil and act exclusively in ways that are beneficial. Naturally, doing so requires courage, which is one of the ingredients in developing stoic fortitude. Most of the time, facing your anxieties and dealing with pain is necessary for doing good. You can only act honorably and pursue your objectives with courage.

You will need the courage to resist when tempted to engage in vice since this will happen frequently. Although vice promises pleasure, that pleasure is fleeting. It always worsens the situation for you and those around you. Contrarily, while virtue may feel difficult at first, its long-term benefits make it worthwhile. If you adopt this attitude, you will be more resilient in difficult situations. You'll discover how to avoid letting the outside world interfere with your ability to make moral decisions.

What do you believe about life, and how does it influence your mental health

and resilience?

To sum up, stoic mental fortitude is concerned with three things:

- letting go of our idealized views of how the world ought to operate and embracing reality.
- remaining unaffected by anything that happens against our choice.
- the willingness to do right.

STOIC WAYS TO OVERCOME THE CHAINS OF THE MODERN WORLD

'If all geniuses in history focused on this one theme, they could never fully explain how baffled they are by the human mind. No one would surrender their estate and the smallest dispute with a neighbor would breed chaos; yet, very easily, we allow others to encroach on our lives. Worse, we create a way for them to take over. No one gives their money to a passerby, but how often do we hand over our lives to others? We hold on to our money and property and think little of wasting time, the one thing we should all be miserly about.'
– Seneca

The modern world has its own chains, even though we may not be someone's slave in the same sense that Epictetus was. Although the scope could extend there, I do not mean a particular religious, cultural, or political system when I refer to shackles in this chapter.

I'm referring to the world that lies beneath it all, the slavery to the whims of our surroundings. I mean, consider the decisions that humanity has made in the past. Everything around us seems to have great control over us. We are content when we achieve our goals.

We feel sad when those items are taken away. We are thrilled when others compliment us. They dislike us, which makes us unhappy.

It appears that the more something we desire, the more willing we are to make sacrifices in order to obtain it. We are more inclined to pay a high price to avoid something the more we reject it. These chains are connected to our preferences and distaste. They manipulate us by instilling fear, placing blame, manipulating us, and making us feel ashamed. As long as we have what they want, they can manipulate us into doing what they want. So we are under the world's control. We turn into the figurative donkey pursuing the carrot on a stick.

We seldom stop to think about whose music we are dancing to as we follow the rider's carrot from conception to death.

But what if we choose to sing our own song instead? What if we refused the carrot and shattered the bonds? The goal of stoicism was to achieve liberation from shackles akin to those found in our world. We do not get that freedom by destroying our surroundings. It's not the environment's fault. Even though we have some control over it, we cannot command the universe; it always does what it does. The conditions of the outside world are imposed upon us in the manner that rain or sunlight affects a farmer's crops. The chains I refer to are not these restrictions. Our ties to them are.

Why is it that anytime something changes at work, we become anxious? Why does it seem that even a minor setback, like someone cutting us off in traffic, can ruin our day? How do the seemingly insignificant twists of fate manipulate our emotions like puppeteers? Death, for instance, is not a bad thing; otherwise, we wouldn't be inspired by the tales of those who bravely faced it, like Socrates. Why are we afraid of it if that is the case? Every time we pull on the chains, they get tighter. We allow luck to rule us whenever we recognize both joy and sorrow in what is natural. Fortunately, the stoics gave us the knowledge to aid in releasing our bonds. Five stoic principles will enable us to replace our irregular way of living with freedom:

Premeditation Malorum: Prepare for the worst

Seneca asserts that the wise person experiences nothing unexpected. Premeditating the worst is a stoic strategy that involves thinking of all the things that could be taken from us or go wrong. This assists you in becoming more resilient when faced with uncertainty and preparing for the setbacks that are unavoidable in life. Sometimes the things we labor so hard for do not come to pass.

Not everything is as easy and positive as we hope. We must therefore be ready for anything.

Seneca continued by saying that we are crushed by the things we do not expect. Their unpredictability gives their misery more weight. Because of this, we ought to avoid being caught off guard by anything. At every turn, practice looking forward with your thoughts. Consider every conceivable scenario. Practice scenarios like a shipwreck, battle, torture, and more in your head. Ensure that you are aware of every aspect of the human experience. You will be ready for difficulty if you do this. You'll be prepared for any outcome.

Think about how everything is interdependent on each other.

The stoics held that everything in the universe is interdependent and interrelated. They are drawn to one another because they are intertwined. According to their relationship and the interconnectedness of all things, one thing follows another. The notion that we are all one is among the most radical stoic concepts. The writings of Seneca, Marcus Aurelius, and Epictetus all contain this connection. In his book Meditations, Marcus Aurelius makes numerous references to the common good.

He views himself as a global citizen as well as a citizen of Rome. The Stoics recognized that they would perform better if they kept in mind the limits of their particular point of view.

In his writings, Marcus Aurelius discussed getting a "view from above." The goal is to fundamentally refute your assumptions. In this manner, you develop a more sympathetic, balanced, and accurate perspective on the world. You can teach yourself how to do this. The suggestion is to take a step back and zoom out so that you can view life from a higher perspective. This is sometimes referred to as "sympathetic." Your value judgments will shift, temptation and luxury will have less control over you, and racial and ethnic disparities will disappear. Additionally, it will lessen your daily worries. Test it out and see.

Keep the ultimate good in mind.

Marcus Aurelius believed that virtue, otherwise known as truth, justice, self-control, and courage, is the highest value in life. The capacity of your intellect is what enables you to make rational decisions and accept the dictates of fate that are beyond your control. You ought to strive to achieve the maximum good in life. The stoics believed that leading a moral life would result in happiness, success, honor, reputation, and a life that had a purpose.

Here, it is not claimed that keeping in mind and following the highest good will be simple. The Stoics didn't believe it would be. In fact, the people around us might not even acknowledge or applaud that approach. However, it is imperative that you are emotionally stable and at peace. The stoics believed that the alternative—following an immoral and unethical path—would only result in sorrow and be fit only for fools and cowards. Your road will be safe if you let virtue guide you at every turn.

The enemy is the ego.

Self-deception, in Zeno's opinion, is the greatest enemy of knowledge. Self-deception and grandiose fantasies are more than just inconveniences and annoyances. Ego is more than just being loud and annoying to be around. It is a sworn adversary of development, education, and advancement. Your inflated sense of self-importance is what prevents you from seeing the truth. It is a visceral form of self-absorption, the idea that you are inherently more entitled and superior to everyone else. One NBA player called the ego the 'disease of me.' It's that inner voice that constantly extols your virtues. Others experience it as the voice that tells them that everyone is against them. The ego is a destructive force that hinders empathy, creativity, openness, and genuine teamwork.

Epictetus contends that no one can learn what he already believes to be true.

You cannot learn, get better, or gain others' respect if you are living in your ego. You consider yourself to be the epitome of perfection and a genius deserving of praise from others. The ego is an enemy of the person you wish you were because of the way it tinkers with your perception of reality. The stoics advised everyone to treat their ego with hatred and contempt. Day by day, we must keep it out of our lives. Just consider it: Can you think of a circumstance in which you would have benefited from having more ego? The ego repels advantages and opportunities while attracting mistakes and errors.

Keeping your ego in check will significantly increase your chances of success in everything you do in life.

Memento Mori: Remember Death

If you've been keeping up with the news, you're aware of all the amazing and occasionally absurd things happening in Silicon Valley.

Recently, one of Peter Thiel's works was constantly making headlines. According to reports, the man is about to discover the secret to eternal life.

Startups will allegedly be successful in bestowing immortality soon enough. According to reports, one man wants to "cure death," while another believes that no one should accept death. These men think that we will not only live forever but also merge with the singularity.

They believe that humanity and artificial intelligence will combine to overcome human limitations. We are frozen in liquid nitrogen and awakened when humanity finally achieves immortality if we do not arrive there quickly enough.

Of course, there is also the skeptics' perspective on the matter. That side has those who do not believe that humans will be merged with computers. The curious thing though is that even that group would still rather avoid thinking about death. To them, it is scary and unpleasant. It is sad. Why would anyone want to think about something they do not want to happen? The truly wise, though, know that both sides are misguided. They have understood that death is not something to be avoided but embraced, so they act according to this truth.

Seneca advised that we prepare our minds for death. Then, we would postpone nothing. He urged us to balance life's books every day so that everyone puts the finishing touches at the end of each day as though it were the last. The ancient Romans had a tradition where they celebrated victorious generals when they returned. The celebration would be a drawn-out spectacle meant to exalt the leader. On the day of the parade, the leader was required to wear a crown and a gold and purple toga that was only reserved for kings.

He would be given a four-horse chariot that would go parting the streets, lined with people chanting about his triumph.

However, in all this pomp and glory, there was also a curious addition. Deliberately positioned in the chariot behind the master, a slave would whisper to him 'Memento mori, memento mori.'

Otherwise translated it means, 'Remember that you are mortal.' The reminder was meant to help the man survive his momentary immortalization without delusions of grandeur.

Lately, people talk about living each day like it was your last so much that it has become cliché. Yet, few people actually live that way, even though that is the essence of remembering death. No, it does not mean that you forsake considerations and laws as if it is the end of the world. What the stoics were saying is that you are a soldier in a battle. You do not know when you will be called to return. You must handle your business. Tell your loved ones that you care. You do not have time to argue over petty issues. You live each day knowing that if it were indeed your last, you would die well.

SO HOW ARE YOU LIVING YOUR LIFE?

When was the last time you contemplated death? The stoics never divorced a good life with thoughtfulness. If you want to escape the chains of the modern world, you have to:

- Pre-meditate the worst.
- Consider how everything is interconnected.
- Pursue the highest good.
- Kill the ego, and Remember death.

AFTERWORD

Few of us consider ourselves to be philosophers. We don't consider ourselves to be anything like the aloof academics in college who would spend countless days researching the philosophical texts by authors like Karl Marx. Thankfully, we don't have to be that way to reap the rewards of applying stoic wisdom to our lives.

Complicated theories about the nature of the universe and how it works are unimportant to stoicism. It all revolves around assisting us in managing negative emotions and conducting ourselves in the most effective manner possible.

I've laid it all out for you in this book. I've tried to be as explicit and actionable as I can be with this. You have a good understanding of how unexpected the world may be and how little power we have over our destiny and our surroundings thanks to this book. You are aware of how brief life is. Only those who are strong and unwavering are able to maximize their time here. Hopefully, you felt that your unhappiness was acknowledged and understood. You now understand that you do not have to live at the whim of your feelings, other people's perceptions, and uncontrollable factors.

Most of the teachings and recommendations are taken from the writings of Marcus Aurelius, Seneca, and Epictetus. There have also been scattered mentions of Zeno the Citium and a few other individuals.

I hope you could understand how stoicism is different from other schools of philosophy in that it emphasizes practical application.

Intelligence is not relevant. It is a tool that you may employ to improve as a parent, a friend, and a person. It's not something to beat yourself up about or use to show off your shortcomings. It has a calming design and a transforming outcome. So, the next question is: Will you actually use what you've learned? Will you add this to your library of information or will you allow it to sift through your heart and alter the way you live? If you let it, the stoics' knowledge found in this book will make your life happier; you'll care less and be able to control your emotions as the stoics did. Good luck on your journey!